THREE ENGLISH STATESMEN.

THREE
ENGLISH STATESMEN:

A COURSE OF LECTURES

ON THE

POLITICAL HISTORY OF ENGLAND.

BY

GOLDWIN SMITH.

Essay Index Reprint Series

BOOKS FOR LIBRARIES PRESS
FREEPORT, NEW YORK

First Published 1867
Reprinted 1972

Library of Congress Cataloging in Publication Data

Smith, Goldwin, 1823-1910.
    Three English statesmen.

    (Essay index reprint series)
    Reprint of the 1867 ed.
    1. Pym, John, 1584-1643. 2. Cromwell, Oliver,
1599-1658. 3. Pitt, William, 1759-1806. I. Title.
DA307.S5 1972   942.06 [B]   72-4587
ISBN 0-8369-2979-9

PRINTED IN THE UNITED STATES OF AMERICA

CONTENTS.

THREE ENGLISH STATESMEN.

I.

PYM.

LET us never glorify revolution. Statesman-ship is the art of avoiding it, and of making progress at once continuous and calm. Revolutions are not only full of all that a good citizen and a good Christian hates while they last, but they leave a long train of bitterness behind. The energy and the exaltation of character which they call forth are paid for in the las-situde, the depression, the political infidelity which ensue. The great spirits of the English Revolution were followed by the men of Charles II. Whatever of moral grandeur there was in the French Revolution was followed by Bonapartism and Talleyrand. Even while the great men are on the scene, violence and one-sidedness mar their greatness. Let us pray that all our political contests may be carried on as the contests of fellow citizen, and beneath the unassailed majesty of law. But the chiefest authors of revolutions have been not the chimerical and intemperate friends of progress, but the blind obstructers of progress; those who, in defiance of nature, struggle to avert the inevitable future, to recall the irrevocable past; who chafe to fury by damming up its course the river which would otherwise flow calmly between its banks, which has ever flowed, and which, do what they will, must flow for ever.

If a revolution ever was redeemed by its grandeur, it was the revolution which was opened by Pym, which was closed by Cromwell, of which Milton was the apostle and the poet. The material forces have been seen in action on a more imposing scale, the moral forces never. Why is that regard for principle, which was so strong among us then, comparatively so weak among us now? The greatest member of parliament that ever lived, the greatest master of the convictions and the feelings of the House of Commons, was not Robert Peel, but John Pym. But if Pym, in modern garb and using modern phrase, could now rise in his old place, his words, though as practical as they are lofty, would, I fear, be thought "too clever for the House." Is it that wealth, too much accumulated and too little diffused, has placed the leadership of the nation in less noble hands ?

We must not regard this revolution merely as the struggle of the English House of Commons against the tyranny of Charles I. It was part of a European conflict between two great opposing currents of opinion, one running towards the future, the other towards the past. The Reformation, like all really great movements, was religious ; but acting on the deepest part of humanity, it impelled forwards the whole nature of man ; and the reaction against it accordingly was a reaction of all the powers of the past. In Spain the reaction, both political and ecclesiastical, had triumphed through the alliance of the Inquisition and the kings. In France the political reaction had triumphed through the policy of Richelieu, whom some, thinking more of organisation than of life, number with the friends of progress ; the rest was to be done by Louis XIV. In Germany, Austria and the Catholic League had nearly crushed the independence of the Protestant states, and made a Catholic empire of the land of Luther. At first the Reformation, with liberty in its train, had spread over all the nations that spoke a Teutonic tongue ; it had spread over a great part of France ; it had gained a footing in Italy and Spain. Now, England and Holland seemed to stand almost alone. It was a crisis as perilous as that of the Armada. How natural to humanity, wearied and perplexed with change, is this yearning for the thrones and for the altars of the past !

In England, however, not only was there this conflict between the Reformation and its enemies. Here, the real reformation was still to come. The reformation of Henry VIII. was a royal reformation, which put the king in the place of the pope. The people were now to have their reformation, a reformation of conviction, which put conscience in the place both of pope and king.

I take for granted a knowledge of the reign of James I. ; the glories of Elizabeth lighting up the shame of her successor; the fatal question whether sovereign power resided with the king or with the parliament, kept undecided by

her tact, forced to decision by his folly; the
weaknesses of a sovereign who seemed born to
advance constitutional liberty by provoking resistance which he could not quell, and proclaiming principles of absolutism which he could not
sustain; the close alliance between prerogative
and the priest party, the king insulting the
Puritan divines at the Hampton Court conference, and the bishops prostrate in grateful
ecstasies at his feet; the government of favourites, whose names were bywords of infamy;
the judicial murder of Raleigh; the disgrace of
Chief Justice Coke, and of the common law in
his person; the divorce of Essex; the murder
of Overbury; the mysterious threats by which
the murderers appealed not in vain to the guilty
conscience of the king; the uprising of the
Commons; the Protestation of Right; the
storm of national resentment to which the court
sacrificed Bacon—Bacon, who served darkness
in the hope that when he had raised himself to
power his science would make the darkness
light, the dupe of a dream of beneficent despotism, a warning to fastidious minds if they
would work for the people to work with and
by the people.

I take for granted, too, a knowledge of the early part of the life and reign of Charles: the ominous episode of the Spanish match; the scenes of duplicity which followed, already revealing the dark spot in Charles's character; the ascendancy of Buckingham, safely intrenched in favour, more safely than ever Strafford was, because his mind was not above that of his master; the coronation, in which the bishops and their paraphernalia played so conspicuous a part; the brief honeymoon of the new king and his parliament; the renewal of the struggle; Charles's policy oscillating between government by parliament and government by prerogative, and both ways fatally to himself; his foreign policy oscillating between the support of Protestant freedom, for which the nation called, and the support of Catholic absolutism, towards which his own heart yearned; the French queen, with her French notions of what a king and a queen should be; the beginnings of arbitrary taxation and military rule; the " great, warm, and ruffling parliament," as Whitelocke calls it, by which those encroachments were withstood; the Petition of Right, that complement of the Great Charter, which declares that Englishmen shall never be subject to martial law, and which if it be tampered with in our day, though it be in the person of the humblest English subject, we purpose, after the example of our great forefathers, to make good.

At last Charles broke with his parliament, passionately dissolved it amidst a scene of tempestuous violence (the Speaker being held down in his chair till the protest of the Commons had been made), and by proclamation forbade any man to talk of a parliament being ever held again. The leader of the Commons, Sir John Eliot, was thrown into the Tower. There he sank at last beneath the bad air and the chills of his prison-house, constantly refusing, as a champion of the law, to do homage to lawlessness by submission. "My lodgings are removed, and I am now where candle-light may be suffered, but scarce fire." So he writes when he is dying of consumption. The court knew what they were doing. "I must tell you," writes Lord Cottington to the renegade Strafford, "that your old, dear friend Sir John Eliot is very like to die." His family petitioned for leave to bury him among his fathers in his Cornish home. The king wrote at the foot of the petition, "Let Sir John Eliot's body be buried in the church of that parish where he died." But Sir John Eliot's spirit rose in the king's path in a decisive hour.

Then followed eleven years of government by prerogative—in place of Parliament, the triune despotism of the Privy Council, the Star Chamber, the Court of High Commission; in place of laws, proclamations; in place of courts of law, courts of arbitrary power; in place of legal taxation by parliament, forced loans, monopolies, feudal and forest extortions, ship-money; the tenure of the judges made during the king's pleasure, that they might be perfect slaves to the king's will; the tamperings with the bench, by which old Judge Whitelocke warned Laud he would in the end raise a flame in the nation; the "Book of Sports" put forth not only to do despite to the Puritan Sabbath, but to make a merry England, free from political thought; the Protestant cause abroad openly abandoned; the strength of the nation declining as the power of the crown rose, and Barbary pirates riding triumphant in the Channel; Strafford and Laud with their policy of Thorough ; Laud, Primate and Chancellor, extirpating freedom of thought in England ; Strafford, lord deputy of Ireland, making ready there an army for the completion of the joint work, and reading us two lessons which. from so able an enemy we shall do well to learn; first, that a standing army is a standing menace to public liberty ; and, secondly, that arbitrary government in a dependency is the stepping-stone to arbitrary government at home. Hopelessly as it seemed at the time, Hampden withstood ship-money : he was cast in his suit before a servile and unjust court, but he proved that in a righteous cause a defeat before an unjust court may be a victory before the people.

With tyranny in the state, tyranny in the church went hand in hand. Intimate is the connection between political freedom and freedom of the soul : eternal is the alliance of the Lauds and the Straffords against both. Reaction in the state and reaction in the church, a Romanising clergy, and a government tending to martial law, these are the joint characteristics not of one age alone. The dry bones of the Tudor episcopate had now begun to live with a portentous life of priestly ambition, the source

of which was Rome, and which soon sought
union with its source. To unprotestantise the
Church of England, Laud laboured with canons
and ordinances, with books and sermons, with
preferments for the compliant, with whips,
pillories, and banishment for recusants, at a
rate which happily for us left prudence as well
as charity and humanity behind. Protestant
preachers were driven from their pulpits, harried
out of the kingdom—among them the favourite
preacher of an obscure sectary named Cromwell. The altar was set up again in place of
the communion table. The eucharistic miracle,
the talisman of priestly power, was again performed. Clerical celibacy, monachism, the con-
fessional, were coming in due course. Persons
of quality especially embraced a religion of
flowers and incense, of millineries and uphol-
steries, of insinuating directors. Only some
spirits, too impatient and too logical, could
not be kept from cutting short the process and
going at once to Rome. The Protestant refugee
churches in England were crushed; it seems
their members kept some trade secrets to themselves, and did not contribute so much as was
to be desired to the wealth of the kingdom.

The communion of the Protestant churches abroad, which Hooker had acknowledged, was renounced, because having no bishops they could not be Christian; and this no doubt was called the reunion of Christendom. To all this the hearty support of the Court was given, and it was well earned. The High Church clergy preached the Loan as vigorously as the Real Presence or the Apostolical Succession. The court divine, Manwaring, said in one of his famous sermons, "that the first of all relations was that between the Creator and the creature; the next between husband and wife; the third between parent and child; the fourth between lord and servant; and that from all these arose that most high, sacred, and transcendent relation between king and subject." In another passage he asks himself "Why religion doth associate God and the king?" and he answers, "that it may be for one of three reasons; because in Scripture the name of god is given to angels, priests, and kings; or from the propinquity of offences against God and his anointed king; or from the parity of beneficence which men enjoy from sacred kings, and which they can no more requite in the case of the king

than in the case of God." He reasons, " that
as justice, properly so called, intercedes not between God and man, nor between the prince,
being a father, and the people as children (for
justice is between equals), so cannot justice be
any rule or medium whereby to give God or
the king his right." And again, he draws a
comparison between the dignity of angels and
that of kings from which it is plain that bishop-
rics are not in the gift of the angels. This
in the Chapel Royal, where, as Pym said, that
doctrine was already so well believed that no
man needed to be converted. Manwaring, Sib-
thorpe, and Montagu belong as yet not wholly
to the past; but the members of the Church
of England have the happiness of knowing that
there are some at least among her clergy in
high places who labour, and labour successfully,
to lay her foundations not in political power
but in the free affection of the people ; to present her as the friend and the consecrator, not
as the enemy, of human progress; and to ally
her not with injustice but with justice.

When Charles dismissed his parliament, the
day was going hard with the Protestant cause
in Germany, the great scene of the conflict, to

which the eyes of all Protestants were wistfully and sadly turned. Tilly and Wallenstein were carrying all before them ; and the last hope of Protestantism seemed to expire when the King of Denmark was overthrown. Suddenly a light shone in the north. Gustavus Adolphus appeared upon the scene. Leipsic, the Gettysburg of the seventeenth century, was fought; and the tidings of a great deliverance and the name of a great deliverer made the heart of the oppressed to leap for joy, and loosened the knees of the oppressor. English and Scottish soldiers of Gustavus, the Garibaldians of their day, came back, not a few to England, many to Scotland, with Garibaldian memories and sentiments in their hearts.

Then Laud laid his rash hand upon the religious independence of Scotland ; and the Scotch nation, nobles and commons, ministers and people, wonderfully fused together by fiery enthusiasm, poured like a lava torrent on the aggressor. English sympathies fought on the Scottish side ; English soldiers refused to conquer for Laud. Strafford's Irish army was not ready. Government by prerogative fell, and Charles called a parliament.

After eleven years without parliaments, most of the members were new. But they had not to seek a leader. They had one whom all accepted in John Pym. Pym had been second only to Sir John Eliot as a leader of the patriot party in the reign of James. He was one of the twelve deputies of the Commons when James cried, with insight as well as spleen, " Set twal chairs ; here be twal kings coming." He had stood among the foremost of those " evil-tempered spirits" who protested that the liberties of parliament were not the favours of the crown, but the birthright of Englishmen, and who for so doing were imprisoned without law. He had resolved, as he said, that he would rather suffer for speaking the truth, than the truth should suffer for want of his speaking. His greatness had increased in the struggle against Charles I. He had been one of the chief managers of the impeachment of Buckingham ; and for that service to public justice, he had again suffered a glorious imprisonment. He had accused Manwaring ; he had raised a voice of power against the Romanising intrigues of Laud. In those days, he and Strafford were dear friends, and fellow soldiers

in the same cause. But when the death of
Buckingham left the place of First Minister
vacant, Strafford sought an interview with Pym
at Greenwich; and when they met began to
talk against dangerous courses, and to hint at
advantageous overtures to be made by the
court. Pym cut him short: "You need not
use all this art to tell me that you have a
mind to leave us. But remember what I tell
you: you are going to be undone. And remember also, that though you leave us, I will
never leave you while your head is upon your
shoulders!" Such at least was the story current in the succeeding age of the last interview
between the Great Champion of Freedom and
the Great Apostate.

Pym was a Somersetshire gentleman of good
family; and it was from good families, such
families at least as do not produce Jacobins,
that most of the leaders of this revolution
sprang. I note it, not to claim for principle
the patronage of birth and wealth, but to show
how strong that principle must have been
which could thus move birth and wealth away
from their natural bias. It is still true, not in
the ascetic, but in the moral sense, that it is

hard for a rich man to enter into the kingdom
of heaven ; and when we see rich men entering
into the kingdom of heaven, hazarding the en-
joyment of wealth for the sake of principle, we
may know that it is no common age.   Oxford
was the place of Pym's education, and there he
was distinguished not only by solid acquire-
ments, but by elegant accomplishments, so that
an Oxford poet calls him the favourite of Apollo.
High culture is now rather in disgrace in some
quarters, and not without a colour of reason,
as unbracing the sinews of action and destroying sympathy with the people.   Nevertheless,
the universities produced the great statesmen
and the great warriors of the Commonwealth.
If the Oxford of Pym, of Hampden, and of
Blake, the Oxford of Wycliffe, the Oxford where
in still earlier times those principles were nursed
which gave us the Great Charter and the House
of Commons—if this Oxford, I say, now seems
by her political bearing to dishonour learning,
and by an ignoble choice does a wrong to
the nation which Lancashire is called upon to
redress—believe me, it is not the University
which thus offends, but a power alien to the
University and alien to learning, to which the

University is, and, unless you rescue her, will continue to be, a slave.

It is another point of difference between the English and the French revolutions that the leaders of the English revolution were as a rule good husbands and fathers, in whom domestic affection was the root of public virtue. Pym, after being for some time in public life, married, and after his marriage lived six years in retirement—a part of training as necessary as action to the depth of character and the power of sustained thought which are the elements of greatness. At the end of the six years his wife died, and he took no other wife but his country.

There were many elements in the patriot party, united at first, afterwards severed from each other by the fierce winnowing-fan of the struggle, and marking by their successive ascendancy the changing phases of the revolution : Constitutional Monarchists, aristocratic Republicans, Republicans thoroughgoing, Protestant Episcopalians, Presbyterians, Independents, and in the abyss beneath them all the Anabaptists, the Fifth Monarchy men, and the Levellers. Pym was a friend of constitutional monarchy in politics, a Protestant Episcopalian in religion ;

against a despot, but for a king; against the
tyranny and the political power of the bishops,
but satisfied with that form of church government. He was no fanatic, and no ascetic. He
was genial, social, even convivial. His enemies
held him up to the hatred of the sectaries as
a man of pleasure. As the statesman and
orator of the less extreme party, and of the first
period of the revolution, he is the English counterpart of Mirabeau, so far as a Christian patriot
can be the counterpart of a Voltairean de-
bauchee.

Nor is he altogether unlike Mirabeau in the
style of his eloquence, our better appreciation of
which, as well as our better knowledge of Pym
and of this the heroic age of our history in
general, we owe to the patriotic and truly
noble diligence of Mr. John Forster, from whose
researches no small portion of my materials
for this lecture is derived. Pym's speeches of
course are seventeenth-century speeches; stately
in diction, somewhat like homilies in their divisions, full of learning, full of Scripture (which
then, be it remembered, was a fresh spring of
new thought), full of philosophic passages which
might have come from the pen of Hooker or of

Bacon. But they sometimes strike the great
strokes for which Mirabeau was famous. Buckingham had pleaded to the charge of enriching
himself by the sale of honours and offices, that
so far from having enriched himself he was
£100,000 in debt. "If this be true," replied
Pym, "how can we hope to satisfy his immense
prodigality ; if false, how can we hope to satisfy
his covetousness ?" In the debate on the Petition of Right, when Secretary Cooke desired in
the name of the king to know whether they
would take the king's word for the observance
of their liberties or not, "there was silence for
a good space," none liking to reject the king's
word, all knowing what that word was worth.
The silence was broken by Pym, who rose and
said, "We have his majesty's coronation oath
to maintain the laws of England ; what need
we then to take his word ?" And the secretary
desperately pressing his point, and asking what
foreigners would think if the people of England
refused to trust their king's word, Pym rejoined,
"Truly, Mr. Secretary, I am of the same opinion
that I was, that the king's oath is as powerful
as his word." In the same debate the courtiers
prayed the House to leave entire his majesty's

sovereign power—a Stuart phrase, meaning the
power of the king when he deemed it expedient
to break the law. " I am not able," was Pym's
reply, " to speak to this question. I know not
what it is. All our petition is for the laws of
England ; and this power seems to be another
power distinct from the power of the law. I
know how to add sovereign to the king's person, but not to his power. We cannot leave
to him a sovereign power, for we never were
possessed of it."

The English Revolution was a revolution of
principle, but of principle couched in precedent.
What the philosophic *salon* was to the French
leaders of opinion, that the historical and an-
tiquarian library of Sir Robert Cotton was to
the English. And of the group of illustrious
men who gathered in that library, none had
been a deeper student of its treasures than
Pym. His speeches and state papers are the
proof.

When the parliament had met, Pym was the
first to rise. We know his appearance from
his portrait—a portly form, which a court
waiting-woman called that of an ox ; a fore-
head so high that lampooners compared it to

a shuttle; the dress of a gentleman of the
time: for not to the cavaliers alone belonged
that picturesque costume and those pointed
beards, which furnish the real explanation of
the fact that all women are Tories. Into the
expectant and wavering, though ardent, minds
of the inexperienced assembly he poured, with
the authority of a veteran chief, a speech which
at once fixed their thoughts, and possessed them
with their mission. It was a broad, complete,
and earnest, though undeclamatory, statement
of the abuses which they had come to reform.
For reform, though for root-and-branch reform,
not for revolution, the Short Parliament came:
and Charles might even now have made his
peace with his people. But Charles did not
yet see the truth: the truth could never pierce
through the divinity that hedged round the
king. The Commons insisted that redress of
grievances should go before supply. In a moment of madness, or what is the same thing,
of compliance with the counsels of Laud, Charles
dissolved the parliament, imprisoned several of
its members, and published his reasons in a proclamation full of despotic doctrine. The friends
of the crown were sad, its enemies very joyful.

Now, to the eye of history, begins to rise that scaffold before Whitehall.

Once more Charles and Strafford tried their desperate arms against the Scotch ; and once more their soldiers refused to fight. Pym and Hampden, meanwhile, sure of the issue, were preparing their party and the nation for the decisive struggle. Their head-quarters were at Pym's house, in Gray's Inn Lane ; but meetings were held also at the houses of leaders in the country, especially for correspondence with the Scotch, with whom these patriot traitors were undoubtedly in league. A private press was actively at work. Pym was not only the orator of his party, but its soul and centre ; he knew how not only to propagate his opinions with words of power, but to organise the means of victory. And now Charles, in extremity, turned to the middle ages for one expedient more, and called a Great Council of Peers, according to Plantagenet precedents, at York. Pym flew at once to York, caused a petition for a parliament to be signed by the peers of his party there, and backed it with petitions from the people, one of them signed by 10,000 citizens of London. This first great wielder of public opinion in England was the inventor of organised agitation by petition. The king surrendered, and called a parliament. Pym and Hampden rode over the country, urging the constituencies to do their duty. The constituencies did their duty, as perhaps they had never done it before, and have never done it since. They sent up the noblest body of men that ever sat in the councils of a nation. The force of the agitation triumphed for the moment, as it did again in 1830, over all those defects in the system of representation which prevail over the public interest and the public sentiment in ordinary times. The Long Parliament met, while round it the tide of national feeling swelled and surged, the long-pent-up voices of national resentment broke forth. It met not for reform, but for revolution. The king did not ride to it in state; he slunk to it in his private barge, like a vanquished and a doomed man.

Charles had called to him Strafford. The earl knew his danger; but the king had pledged to him the royal word that not a hair of his head should be touched. He came foiled, broken by disease, but still resolute, prepared to act on the aggressive, perhaps to arraign the leaders of the Commons for treasonable correspondence with the Scotch. But he had to deal, in his friend and coadjutor of former days, with no mere rhetorician, but with a man of action as sagacious and as intrepid as himself. Pym at once struck a blow which proved him a master of revolution. Announcing to the Commons that he had weighty matter to impart, he moved that the doors should be closed. When they were opened, he carried up to the Lords the impeachment of the Earl of Strafford. The earl came down to the House of Lords that day with his brow of imperial gloom, his impetuous step, his tones and gestures of command: but scarcely had he entered the house when he found that power had departed from him; and the terrible grand vizier of government by prerogative went away a fallen man, none unbonneting to him, in whose presence an hour before no man would have stood covered. The speech by which Pym swept the house on to this bold move, so that, as Clarendon says, " not one man was found to stop the torrent," is known only from Clarendon's outline. But that outline shows how the speaker filled the thoughts of his hearers with a picture of the tyranny, before he named its chief author, the Earl of Strafford; and how he blended with the elements of indignation some lighter passages of the earl's vanity and amours, to mingle indignation with contempt and to banish fear.

Through the report of the Scotch Commissioner Baillie. we see the great trial, to which that of Warren Hastings was a parallel in splendour, but no parallel in interest—Westminster Hall filled with the Peers, the Commons, the foreign nobility, come to learn if they could a lesson in English politics—the ladies of quality, whose hearts (and we can pardon them) were all with the great criminal who made so gallant and skilful a fight for life, and of whom it was said that, like Ulysses, he had not beauty, but he had the eloquence which moved a goddess to love. Among the mass of the audience the interest, intense at first, flagged as the immense process went on; and eating, drinking, loud talking filled the intervals of the trial. But there was one whose interest did not flag. The royal throne was set for the king in his place; but the king was not there.

He was with his queen in a private gallery,
the lattice-work of which, in his eagerness to
hear, he broke through with his own hands.
And there he heard, among other things, these
words of Pym : "If the histories of eastern
countries be pursued, whose princes order their
affairs according to the mischievous principles
of the Earl of· Strafford, loose and absolved
from all rules of government, they will be
found to be frequent in combustions, full of
massacres and of the tragical ends of princes."

I need not make selections from a speech
so well known as that of Pym on the trial of
Strafford. But hear one or two answers to fallacies which are not quite dead yet. To the
charge of arbitrary government in Ireland,
Strafford had pleaded that the Irish were a
conquered nation. "They were a conquered
nation," cries Pym. "There cannot be a word
more pregnant or fruitful in treason than that
word is. There are few nations in the world
that have not been conquered, and no doubt but
the conqueror may give what law he pleases
to those that are conquered; but if the succeeding pacts and agreements do not limit and restrain that right, what people can be secure ?

England hath been conquered, and Wales hath been conquered; and by this reason will be in little better case than Ireland. If the king by the right of a conqueror gives laws to his people, shall not the people, by the same reason, be restored to the right of the conquered to recover their liberty if they can?" Strafford had alleged good intentions as an excuse for his evil counsels. "Sometimes, my lords," says Pym, "good and evil, truth and falsehood, lie so near together that they are hard to be distinguished. Matters hurtful and dangerous may be accompanied with such circumstances as may make them appear useful and convenient. But where the matters propounded are evil in their own nature, such as the matters are wherewith the Earl of Strafford is charged. as to break public faith and to subvert laws and government, they can never be justified by any intentions, how good soever they be pretended." Again, to the plea that it was a time of great danger and necessity, Pym replies: "If there were any necessity, it was of his own making; he, by his evil counsel, had brought the king into a necessity; and by no rules of justice can be allowed to gain this advantage by his own fault, as to make that a

ground of his justification which is a great part
of his offence."

Once we are told, while Pym was speaking,
his eyes met those of Strafford, and the speaker
grew confused, lost the thread of his discourse,
broke down beneath the haggard glance of his
old friend.   Let us never glorify revolution !

It is commonly said that Pym and Hampden,
finding that the evidence for the impeachment
had failed, made short work with their victim
by an Act of Attainder.   Mr. Forster has discovered proof that Pym and Hampden were
personally against resorting to an Act of Attainder, and in favour of praying judgment on
the evidence in the regular way ; but the opinion
of the majority being opposed to theirs, they
went with the rest.   Guilty of treason against
the king Strafford was not, for the king was his
accomplice.   But he was guilty, and he stood
and stands clearly convicted of that which Pym
charged him—treason against the nation.   He
had "endeavoured by his words, actions, and
counsels, to subvert the fundamental laws of
England and Ireland, and to introduce an arbitrary and tyrannical government."   The Act
of Attainder was not in those days what it would

be in ours, an instrument of which no just man
would make use against the worst and most
dangerous of criminals. It had a place in jurisprudence, and would have been used on the like
occasion as freely by one party as by the other.
In this case the process had been perfectly judicial, and the Act of Attainder did no more
than punish treason against the nation, as the
Statute of Treasons would have punished treason
against the king. " Shall it be treason," asked
Pym, alluding to that statute, " to embase the
king's coin, though but a piece of twelvepence
or sixpence ; and must it not needs be the effect
of a greater treason to embase the spirit of his
subjects, and to set a stamp and character of
servitude on them, whereby they shall be disabled to do anything for the service of the
king and the commonwealth ?" And he justly
reasoned that laws would be vain if they had
not a power to preserve themselves, if any aspirant to arbitrary power might with impunity
compass their subversion. Falkland voted for
the Act of Attainder, and Falkland would not
have voted for legislative murder.

The Lords hesitated ; left to themselves they
would have shrunk from convicting on a capital

charge. But the popular clamour was loud and terrible. The Lords showed what in them is called tact, and the Bill of Attainder passed.

The king had pledged his word that not a hair of Strafford's head should be harmed ; and to a chivalrous mind the release which Strafford sent him would have made the pledge doubly strong. But the king had casuists about him, and the queen hated Strafford as the rival of her power, though she allowed that he had fine hands. Before the trial, Charles had attempted to save his minister by making overtures to the leaders of the opposition, which, as they would have come in as a party on their own principles and with full securities, they were not only entitled but bound as an opposition to accept. But the negociation was broken off by Bedford's death. Charles still tried influence and entreaty. But the discovery of the queen's plot (for hers it probably was), to bring up the army and overawe the parliament, sealed Strafford's doom. And so that promise made in the conference at Greenwich was kept to the letter. Better had it not been so. Better to have been satisfied with establishing the principle that treason against the nation was as high

a crime as treason against the king, and then
to have exalted and hallowed the national
cause by mercy. The other course exalted and
half hallowed the crime. But it seems to have
been the feeling of all patriots that the constitution could not be safe while Strafford lived.
It was the moderate and chivalrous Essex that
uttered the hard words—" Stone dead hath no
fellow." Falkland was a party to the death of
Strafford; so was Hyde, who, while he labours
to create the contrary impression, unwittingly
betrays himself by a subsequent admission, that
throughout these transactions he and Falkland
had never differed from each other. So was
Lord Capel, though afterwards, when all was
changed, himself dying as a royalist on the
scaffold, he professed to repent of his vote.

Laud was impeached also. Surely no man
ever tried the sufferance of· his kind more
severely than this persecutor in the name of
an authority which was itself the rebel of yesterday. There is something singularly tyrannical in High Anglican pretensions. The victims of Laud had seen with their own eyes the
introduction of the doctrines and the practices
which they were called upon to accept as the

immemorial and unbroken tradition of an immutable and infallible church. Laud had learnt
government in the petty despotism of a college. He was subject, as his friends said, to
some infirmities of temper; "that is," remarks
Mr. Hallam, "he was choleric, harsh, vindictive,
and even cruel to a great degree." In the case
of Felton he wished to revive the use of torture ; but this was too much, even for the
judges of Charles I. Clarendon tries to make
out that he suffered for his impartial severity
to the vices of the great. No doubt he was
rude, rude as he would have been to college
undergraduates, to all orders of men, and he
made himself some enemies of rank thereby.
But he rose in life as the creature and parasite
of Buckingham. He tried, say High Church
writers, with complacency, to win Buckingham
to the Church's·cause. To the Church's cause,
no ; but to some cause which needs the patronage of Buckinghams. Which element pre-
dominated in his character, that of the bigoted
and intolerant priest, or that of the ecclesiastical
adventurer, it is not easy to say : perhaps the
Roman archives, when they are explored, may
throw some light upon the subject. No man

ever so distinctly conceived the alliance between civil and ecclesiastical tyranny. Who could conceive it so distinctly as the ambitious head of a hierarchy which was a creature of the state? When he had got the great political offices placed in clerical hands, he thought that all that man could do had been done for the Church of God. Over the porch of St. Mary's Church at Oxford stand a Virgin and Child, placed there by Laud. The Virgin she seems to be; but look closer, the circlet round her head is not a heavenly crown, but the coronet of a peeress. She is Political Religion, and in her arms she bears the infant Unbelief.

Pym spoke of course in support of the impeachment of Laud. He denounced in language strong but not virulent the perversion of God's law to defend the lawlessness of man, the abuse of the ministry ordained for the instruction of souls to the promotion of violence and oppression. He remarked that "those who laboured in civil matters to set up the king above the laws of the kingdom, did yet in ecclesiastical matters labour to set up themselves above the king." Laud was consigned to the Tower; but no further proceedings were taken against

him till the hand of death was on Pym ; and
I am persuaded that had Pym lived, Laud
would not have died. It was the narrower
and more cruel Presbyterians that brought the
old man to the block.

And now that promise of a clean sweeping
of the house from floor to roof, which Pym
whispered in Clarendon's ear at the meeting
of the parliament, was vigorously kept. All
the engines of the tyranny were demolished ;
all its chief agents deprived and banished.
The return to government without parliaments
was barred by the Triennial Act. Ship-money
judges learnt, and bequeathed to all who might
like them be tempted to pervert law to the
purposes of power, the lesson that the justice
of a nation, though it sleeps, may not be dead.
A doubt was raised whether the king would
consent to the punishment of so many and such
high delinquents. "Shall we therefore doubt
of justice," said Pym, "because we have need
of great justice ?"

It is mournful to say that one of the complaints against the king was his lenity to Popish
priests. But in him, the persecutor of the Puritans, this lenity was not toleration, but con-

nivance. When the law, hateful as it was, was asserted, and the priests were left to the Commons, their lives were safe—safer, as Clarendon peevishly says, than if they had been pardoned under the great seal. Pym declared expressly that he did not desire any new laws against Popery, or any rigorous courses in the execution of those already in force : he was far from seeking the ruin of their persons or estates ; only he wished they might be kept in such a condition as to restrain them from doing hurt. To restrain them from doing hurt was unhappily in those days part of a statesman's duty. They were liegemen and soldiers of that successor of the apostles whose confederates were Philip II. and Charles IX., and who struck a medal in honour of the massacre of St. Bartholomew.

And now, all these reforms having been accomplished, all these offenders punished, all these securities for lawful government provided, the king having even assented to the act which, in clear contradiction to his prerogative, forbade the dissolution of the then parliament without its own consent, was it not time to bring the movement to a close, and to replace the sovereign power, which the parliament had virtually

seized, in the king's hands ? So thought many
who had up to this point been zealous reformers, and some, at all events, whose opinions
we are bound to treat with respect. So thought
not Pym and Hampden. To them it seemed
that the king could not be trusted; that the
last day of the parliament would be the last of
his good faith; that they must go on till they
had left him no power to undo the work· which
had been done. They remembered the double
answer to the Petition of Right. They remembered, as they showed on all occasions, the
fate of Sir John Eliot. We have good reason,
they perhaps had better reason, to believe that
the court was still hostile, still intriguing, still
aiming at a counter revolution; and Clarendon
owns that Charles had been persuaded to consent to measures which he abhorred, on the
ground that they might be afterwards revoked
on the plea of duress. To the last it proved
hard to bind this anointed king. But let us
not forget to say emphatically, that the leaders
of the Commons needed all this to justify them
in giving the word for revolution.

They prepared a great appeal to the nation,
which took the shape of the Grand Remon-

strance. Charles now went to Scotland, osten-
sibly to settle matters there and disband the
armies, really to make himself a party, and pro-
vide himself with weapons against the leaders
of the opposition. Episcopacy being at this
time threatened with abolition, he assured its
friends that if they could keep the church safe
during his absence, he would undertake for its
safety on his return. Hampden went, with other
delegates of the parliament, to watch him, while
Pym remained at the centre of affairs, one proof
among many that able, powerful, and revered as
Hampden was, Pym, not Hampden, was the real
chief. The higher social position of Hampden
is perhaps the main source of the contrary impression. King Pym was the name given to
Pym by the lampooners, and though in jest they
spoke the truth. "The most popular man," says
Clarendon, "and the most able to do hurt, that
hath lived in any time." The most able to do
hurt, that is the phrase : how can a leader of
the people use his power for good ? And now
came the sinister news of the attempt to make
away with or kidnap the covenanting chiefs in
Scotland ; and close upon it, at once terrible
and maddening to Protestant hearts, the tidings

of the rising of the Catholics and of the massacre of the Protestants in Ireland. The king was innocent of the Irish rebellion ; it was simply a natural episode in the Irish land question. But he wrote to Secretary Nicholas, " I hope this ill news of Ireland will hinder some of those follies in England."

It did not hinder the preparation of the Grand Remonstrance. But a chivalrous royalist tried to hinder all the follies in a more practical way. A letter was one day delivered to Pym in the house by a messenger who had received it from a horseman in gray. When it was opened, there dropt from it a rag which had been taken from a plague sore, and was of course full of infection. The writer intimated that, if this did not do the business, a surer weapon would be tried. A surer weapon, it seems, was tried, but it struck the wrong man. The world improves, though slowly. Then it was the stab of the assassin's dagger ; now it is only the stab of the assassin's tongue.

And now the Grand Remonstrance was ready. Manifestly drawn by Pym, it recites through a long series of clauses, but with monumental gravity and terseness, the grievances for which parliament had extorted redress, and concludes, in effect, by calling on the nation to support its leaders in making the work good against evil counsellors and reaction. On the morning of the 23rd of November, 1641, it lay engrossed upon the table of the House of Commons ; not the present House of Commons, as Mr. Forster reminds us, but the narrow, ill-lighted, dingy room in which for centuries some of the world's most important work was done. And never, perhaps, did that old room, never did any hall of debate, witness such an oratoric struggle as the debate on the Grand Remonstrance. The speakers were Pym, Hampden, Falkland, Hyde, Culpepper, Orlando Bridgman, Denzil Hollis, Waller, Glyn, Maynard, others of name. The stake was the Revolution and the fortunes of all who were embarked in it. Cromwell said that if they had lost he would have left England. The forces were by this time evenly balanced, for secession to the court had made great gaps in the patriot array, and in the royalist ranks were now seen not only Digby, Hyde, Culpepper, but Falkland—Falkland, in whose house, the free resort of all learning, a college, as his friend calls it, situated in a purer air, no small part, perhaps, of the intellectual elements of the revolution had been formed. There were many waverers whose votes were still to be lost or won. From noon to past midnight the battle raged; for a battle it was of orators, not dictating pamphlets to the reporters, but grappling with each other for victory. The merest skeleton, alas! of the speeches alone remains. Pym rose when the debate was at its height, replying to the leaders on the king's side—Hyde, Falkland, Culpepper, and Sir Edward Dering. That the house was thinned by fatigue before the division has been proved to be a mistake; though there were many trimmers who stayed away altogether. At midnight, the Remonstrance was carried by eleven—159 to 148. So charged was the air with the electricity of that fierce debate, that when the royalist Palmer attempted to protest, a tumult arose in which, as one who was present says, they had almost sheathed their swords in each others' breasts. In the following days the exasperated majority proceeded to violent measures against members of the minority. Let us never glorify revolution!

Now Charles arrived from Scotland, inflamed

by contact with the fiery spirit of Montrose, and
bringing the proofs he had sought of the complicity of the oppositior leaders with the Scotch.
He found the royalist reaction strong, many
gained over by the queen, the students of the
Temple hot in his favour, a royalist lórd mayor,
who got up for him an enthusiastic reception
in the city. He was in an atmosphere of
violence. Whitehall was thronged with disbanded officers and soldiers, ready at his command to fall on. The parliament, by a bold act
of sovereign power, had raised for itself a guard.
Soon the names of Cavalier and Roundhead
were heard ; soon blood was shed, and the hand
which unfolds the book of history turned the
red page of civil war. The French queen,
ignorant that in England a nation lay behind
the parliament, thought the time had come for
crushing the ringleaders and stamping out the
revolution. Even now it seems Charles wavered
between two policies, and made some overtures
to Pym. Then he gave ear to the queen and
Digby, impeached the five members, and went
himself, with an armed train, to seize them in
the House of Commons. All know how the
attempt was foiled ; how Lady Carlyle—a

storm-bird of this revolutionary storm, the
political devotee first of Strafford, and when
Strafford fell, of his conqueror—conveyed a
warning to Pym ; how the queen cried joyfully
that the king was master again of his kingdom, and found that she had spoken too soon ;
how Charles entered the house, looked towards
the place, on the right hand near the bar, where
Pym sat, found that he and all the " birds" were
" flown ;" left the house amid cries of " Privilege ;" tried the city ; found there now, instead
of an enthusiastic greeting, shouts of " To your
tents, O Israel ;" and departed from Whitehall,
to return once more ; how the five members
were brought back in triumph, " and," as Clarendon says, with an irony too near the truth, " set
upon their thrones again ;" and how four thousand freeholders of Buckinghamshire rode up to
protect their Hampden. Where are those four
thousand freeholders of Buckinghamshire now ?
And where then our English Hampden stood,
speaking for English liberty, who stands now
upholding martial law as the suspension of all
law ?

Pym must now have seen that he had to
conduct a civil war. His first task was to

strengthen the weak knees of the Lords. The special grievance of the Lords, the preference óf upstart ecclesiastics to the great nobility in appointments to the offices of state, had long ago been redressed ; they saw that matters were going too far for an aristocracy, and they had begun by their qualms greatly to disturb the unity of action. They had thrown out the bill for taking away the votes of the bishops. A great popular demonstration was got up against obstruction. Pym carried the petitions of the people to the Lords, and backed them with a speech, in which he said that the Commons "would be sorry that the story of that parliament should tell posterity that in so great a danger and extremity the House of Commons should be enforced to save the kingdom alone." The Lords again showed tact ; they passed the bishops' bill with only three dissentient voices, and they also passed the bill giving parliament the command of the militia.

The passing of the bill for taking away the bishops' votes was a matter of vital necessity to Pym, who though himself, as has been said already, an Episcopalian, and the reverse of a fanatic, was thrown more and more, as the struggle went on and the moderates seceded, on the Presbyterians and the Independents. From the Independents we may be sure his cultivated statesmanship would shrink ; but as a leader he must have noted that the unwavering courage and devotion of these men, their fixity of purpose, their terrible force, stood out more clearly as the sky darkened and the storm came on. Mirabeau marked the intensity of conviction which was to give ultimate ascendancy to the chief of the Jacobins. Pym may have marked the same thing in Cromwell.

The final rupture between the king and the Commons took place on the demand of the parliament for the control of the military forces of the kingdom. No doubt if Charles had yielded to this demand, nothing would have been left him but the name and state of a king. And yet while the king had the power of the sword, could a constitution which he desired to overthrow be secure ? The question is not made less grave by the substitution of a standing army for a militia. It may one day present itself again. In truth it does partly present itself whenever an attempt is made to bring the Horse Guards under constitutional control.

A pause ensues of eight months, during which all Englishmen are choosing their parts, all preparing for civil war ; the king's pursuivants and his commissions of array are being encountered by the commissioners and the ordinances of the parliament ; the old corselet and steel-cap, the old pike, and sword, and carbine are being taken down from the wall where they had hung since the time of the Armada ; the hunter and the farmhorse are being trained to stand fire ; squadrons of yeomen, battalions of burghers are being drilled by officers who had served under Gustavus ; French and German engineers are organising the artillery ; uniforms are being made for Newcastle's white-coats, Hampden's green-coats, Lord Saye's blue-coats, the City of London's red-coats ; banners are being embroidered with mottoes, loyal or patriotic ; friends who have taken opposite sides with sad hearts are waving a last farewell across the widening gulf to each other. Sir William Waller, the parliamentarian general, writes to his future antagonist, the royalist general, Sir Ralph Hopton : " My affections to you are so unchangeable, that hostility itself cannot violate my friendship to your person ; but I must be true to the cause wherein I serve.

The great God, who is the searcher of my heart,
knows with what reluctance I go upon this
service, and with what perfect hatred I look
upon a war without an enemy. The God of
peace in his good time send us peace, and in
the meantime fit us to receive it. We are both
on the stage, and we must act the parts that
are assigned us in this tragedy. Let us do it
in a way of honour, and without personal ani-
mosities." Not only friend against friend, neighbour against neighbour, but father against son,
son against father, brother against brother,
women's hearts torn between the husband who
fought on one side, the father and brother who
fought on the other ; those who last Christmas
met round the same board, before next Christmas
to meet in battle. If the High Church bishops
and clergy were too roughly handled, as unhappily they were, let it be remembered that
this was their war. It was truly called Bellum
Episcopale. "I have eaten the king's bread,"
said Sir Edmund Verney, the king's standard-
bearer, "near thirty years, and I will not do
so base a thing as to forsake him. I choose
rather to lose my life (which I am sure I shall
do) to preserve and defend those things which

are against my conscience to preserve and defend;
for I will deal freely with you, I have no reverence for the bishops, for whom this quarrel
subsists." Sir Edmund's presentiment was true:
the first battle released him from this struggle
between his conscience and his chivalry.

Let it be noted, however, that the injunction
of Sir William Waller was not unobserved.
This war was on the whole carried on in a way
of honour; and if not without personal ani-
mosity, at least without the savage cruelty
which has marked the civil wars of some nations. It was waged like a war of principle,
like the war of a self-controlled and manly race.
It was entered upon too, by the Commons at
least, in the right spirit, as a most mournful
necessity, with public humiliation and prayer.
The playhouses were closed by an ordinance of
the Parliament as in a time of national sorrow.
These hypocrites, say royalists, knelt down to
pray, and rose up again to shed innocent blood.
And does not every religious soldier, when he
goes into battle, do the same?

The king had now on his side almost all the
nobility, most of the wealthier gentry, and the
more backward parts of the country, in which

the feudal tie between the landowners and the
peasantry was still strong ; such as the western
counties, Wales, and part of the north. Of
course he had the Episcopalian clergy, and the
cathedral towns and universities which were
under their influence. Oxford, once the intellectual head-quarters of Simon de Montfort,
was now the head-quarters of Charles. The
Roman Catholics also were with him ; he and
they were in the same plot against liberty,
though they did not yet quite understand each
other. Pym and the Commons were strong
in the more advanced and commercial districts,
especially in the eastern counties. They had
all the great towns, even those in the districts
favourable to the enemy. " The town of Manchester," says Clarendon, " had from the beginning, out of that factious humour which
possessed most corporations, and the pride of
their wealth, opposed the king, and declared
magisterially for the parliament." Birmingham,
too, according to the same authority, " was of
as great fame for hearty, wilful, affected dis-
loyalty to the king as any place in England."
London was the head-quarters ; not a London
of warehouses at one end and Belgravias at

the other, but a great city democracy, still warlike, as the conduct of the train-bands at Newbury proved, and devoted with heart and purse to the cause. Above all, the Commons had the lesser gentry and the independent yeomanry, everywhere attached to the cause by its religious side. Those independent yeomanry, with high hearts and convictions of their own, who filled the ranks of the Ironsides, who conquered for English liberty at Marston, Naseby, and Worcester, in their native England are now seen no more. Here they have left a great, perhaps a fatal, gap in the ranks of freedom. But under Grant and Sherman they still conquer for the good cause.

Foreign powers stood neutral. Happily for us, Laud's desire of reunion with Rome had not been fulfilled, and the Anglican reaction in England remained isolated from the Catholic reaction in the rest of Europe. The Anglican Pope could not stoop to submission, and Rome would hear of no compromise. To all offers of compromise, to all offers of anything but submission, she then said *non possumus*, and she says *non possumus* still. So the Catholic powers left Charles to the doom of a heretic

E

prince, and when his head fell on the scaffold, took the opportunity of buying his fine collection of works of art. Spain played her own game in Ireland; and Richelieu throughout the whole of these transactions had been intriguing with the leaders of the Commons. The sympathies of the States of Holland were with the parliament, those of the House of Orange with the king.

Standing army in those days there was none; if there had been, Charles would have crushed liberty. The navy was on the side of the Commons. The sailors were inclined to Puritanism, and they were the sons of those who had fought against the Armada.

The voice of the cannon was heralded by volleys of paper missiles from both sides. This is the stormy birth-hour of our newspaper press; and it is instructive to see that, from the first, the party of "blood and culture" held its own in ruffianism and ribaldry. A statelier war of manifestoes meanwhile was waged between Pym in the name of the Commons, and Clarendon in the name of the king. Hallam thinks that Clarendon had the best of it. Mr. Forster scouts the idea. But I am of

Hallam's mind. Pym is trying to make the
parchment of legality cover a revolution ; and
so stretched, the parchment cracks, as Clarendon
does not fail to mark. Yet Pym was wise in
presenting his cause as legally as possible to a
law-loving people, who had not learnt to think
of law apart from a king. Nor does he fail to
display his power, which lay especially in un-
masking fallacies of principle. Hyde had argued
that the king had as good a title to his town
of Hull and its magazines, as any of his subjects had to their houses and lands, and that
to dispose of the place without his consent
would shake the foundations of property in
general. " Here," replies Pym, "that is laid
down for a principle which would indeed pull
up the very foundation of the liberty, property,
and interest of every subject in particular, and
of all the subjects in general, if we should
admit it for a truth that his majesty hath the
same right and title to his towns and magazines (bought with the public money, as we
conceive that at Hull to have been) that every
particular man hath to his house, lands, and
goods ; for his majesty's towns are no more
his own than his people are his own ; and if

the king had a property in all his towns, what
would become of the subjects' property in their
houses therein ?"

A provisional government of five peers and
ten commoners was formed, under the name of
the Committee of Safety, and installed at Derby
House. At its head was Pym. Hampden went
down to his county to muster his yeomen, and
to second and perhaps watch Essex, a military
grandee of rather lukewarm sentiments, though
honourable and trustworthy, whom it was
thought politic to make commander-in-chief.
Pym in his youth had been in the Exchequer ;
and the Chancellorship of the Exchequer was
the office destined for him when he and his
friends were on the point of forming a government. He now used his financial knowledge
to organise the finance of the Commons in the
way of regular taxation extending over all the
districts in their power, to the envy of Clarendon, whose side was supplied only by irregular
contributions and by the rapine, as wasteful as
it was odious, of Rupert. "One side," says
Clarendon, mournfully, "seemed to fight for
monarchy with the weapons of confusion, and
the other to destroy the king and government

with all the principles and regularity of monarchy."

Towards the end of October, 1642, whatever there may have been on Pym's brow, deep care must have been in his heart, for the king was moving southwards on London, Essex was wait-ing on his march, and a battle was at hand. Accordingly, on Monday, the 24th, came first, borne on the wings of fear, the news of a great defeat; then better news, then worse news again; then Lord Wharton and Mr. Strode from the army, with authentic tidings of the doubtful victory of Edgehill. Edgehill, the king's evening halting-place, looks out from the brow of the high table-land on a wide cham-paign; and immediately below lies the little town of Keynton, the evening halting-place of Essex. Between Edgehill and Keynton is a wood called the Graves, the burial-place of five thousand Englishmen slain by English hands, among them it was said of a soldier to whom death was made more bitter by the thought that he had fallen by the carbine, in vain avoided, of his brother. There, on the Sabbath day, October 23, Roundhead and Ca-valier first tried the bitter taste of civil war.

From two o'clock till nightfall the plain between Edgehill foot and Keynton was filled
with the wild and confused eddies of a battle
fought by raw troops under inexperienced commanders.   The action was, however, a sort of
epitome of the war.   It began with the deser-
tion to the enemy of a body of Parliamentary
horse under Fortescue, named by his sponsors,
in prophetic irony, Sir Faithful.   Rupert with
his cavalry carried all before him, rode headlong
off in pursuit, and returned with his wearied
horsemen to find the Parliamentary infantry in
possession of the field, and the king's person
in great danger.   The army of the Commons
was enabled to hold its ground that night and
the next day, and thus to gain the semblance
of a victory—a semblance which was the saving
of the cause—by the zeal of the country people,
who eagerly brought them provisions, while the
king's soldiers, when they went out to forage,
were knocked upon the head.   But as yet there
was no Cromwell in command, and the serving-
men and tapsters in the army were too many,
the Ironsides were too few, as in the Federal
army at Bull's Run there was too much of
New York and too little of Illinois.   Edgehill

was, in fact, our Bull's Run. The panic of the
Parliamentary horse at the first charge of the
Cavaliers was shameful. Some must have fled
still earlier, if there be any truth in Clarendon's
statement that though the battle began so late,
runaways, and not only common soldiers, but
officers of rank, were in St. Albans before nightfall. If the *Times'* correspondent had been
there, he would certainly have reported that
Englishmen would not fight. Our nation, like
the American nation of late, had to go through
greater trials, and be thrown more upon its
nobler self, before it could deserve victory.

The Commons voted Essex £5,000 for his
success. But meanwhile the king was taking
Banbury, and in a fortnight he was before
London. The Commons had gone into the conflict, like the people of the Northern States, full
of overweening confidence in their superior numbers and resources, and ignorant of the bitterness
of war. They had now found to their cost that
an aristocracy and its dependants, used, the
m sters to command and the servants to obey,
have a great advantage over a democracy in the
field, till the democracy have learnt the higher
discipline of intelligent submission to command

for the sake of their own cause. From the pinnacle of exaltation they fell into the depth of discouragement; and the thirteen months of life which remained to Pym were months of incessant struggle against despondency, defection, and disaster. The peers soon began to fall away. The few members of the Upper House who stayed at Westminster were a perpetual source of timid councils. Essex himself, though he kept his faith, felt the bias of his order; he was at best far from a great general, and his operations in the field were apt to be affected by fits of political moderation. The fortune of war was on the whole decidedly in favour of the king. The Fairfaxes were defeated at Atherton. Sir William Waller, after the brief career of victory which gained him the nickname of William the Conqueror, met with a bloody and decisive overthrow at Roundway Down. Bristol was surrendered by Fiennes, the only notable instance of a want of military courage among these leaders who, many of them so late in life, had changed peaceful arts for war. Only in the association of the eastern counties, where Cromwell fought under Lord Mandeville, the light of hope still shone. The

discovery of the plot formed by Waller, who
had been a leading patriot in the debate on the
Grand Remonstrance, to deliver London to the
king, revealed the abyss on the edge of which
the leaders of the Commons stood. A mob of
women, and women in men's clothes, came to the
House of Commons, calling for the traitor Pym,
and it was necessary to disperse them with
cavalry. Hampden, Pym's second self, and the
second pillar of the cause, fell in a petty skirmish
on Chalgrove Field. Yet Pym seems to have
remained master of the burning vessel, tossed
as she was upon a raging sea. He managed
the war, kept watch against conspiracy, held
together the discordant and wavering party in
parliament, sustained by his eloquence the enthusiasm of the city. Unable to quell the
tendency of the peace party to treat, he adroitly
fell in with it ; went down himself to the city,
which had become infuriated at the report of
negociations, to vindicate the character of the
parliament, and thus remaining master of the
negociations, prevented them from degenerating
into surrender. While the king, made confident
by success, was issuing proclamations promising
pardon to all but leading rebels, Pym daringly

impeached the queen for the part which she was taking in the war. The queen was not in his hands, nor likely to be ; and if she had been she would have been safe. The move was intended only to commit Parliament past recall, and to hurl defiance at the king. The Presbyterians were secured by the appointment of the Assembly of Divines to reform the church after their model. But it is evident that the free nature of Pym, and the free natures of other men like Pym, struggled hard and long before they could consent to bow their necks to the yoke of the Calvinistic covenant, on which condition alone the aid, now indispensable, could be obtained from the Scotch.

The tide still ran for the king. Gloucester, the last stronghold of the Commons in the west, was in peril. Essex had sent to the Houses proposals for an accommodation, the rejection of which Pym and St. John, by their utmost efforts, could only just procure. Then Pym went down to the tent of Essex, tried on the moody and jealous aristocrat the powers of persuasion which had carried the Grand Remonstrance, and tried them not in vain. Essex marched ; Gloucester was relieved ; the king was worsted at Newbury; and a ray of victory, breaking from the cloud, shone upon Pym's last hour.

Work tells upon the sensitive organisations of men of genius. Pym had been working, as the preacher of his funeral sermon tells us, from three in the morning till evening, and from evening again till midnight. He must have borne a crushing weight of anxiety besides. The loathsome fables invented by the royalists are not needed to account for the failure of his health. He met his end, if we may trust the report of his friends, with perfect calmness. At the last, we are told, he fell into a swoon, and when he recovered his consciousness, seeing his friends weeping round him, he told them that he had looked death in the face, and therefore feared not the worst he could do; added some words of religious hope and comfort; and, while a minister was praying with him, quietly slept with God. Funeral sermons are not history. No character is flawless, least of all the characters of men who lead in violent times. But if the cause of English liberty was a good cause, Pym's conscience, so far as we can see, might well bid him turn calmly to his rest.

The King of the Commons was buried with the utmost pomp and magnificence in the resting-place of kings. The body was borne from Derby House to Westminster Abbey by ten of the leading members of the House of Commons, followed by both Houses of Parliament in full mourning, by the Assembly of Divines, and by many gentlemen of quality, with two heralds of arms before the corpse bearing the crest of the deceased. This last piece of state shows how near we still are to feudalism, how far from the *Sans-culottes*. Ten thousand pounds were voted to pay Pym's debts, a proof that he had not grown rich by the public service. No doubt he had been obliged to keep some state and hospitality, as head of the provisional government, at Derby House. A pension was also voted to his son, who bore arms for the parliament, but after the Restoration sank into a baronetcy—one proof among many that public virtue is not hereditary, and that its titles ought not to be so. Nor did Oxford fail in its way to do honour to the departed chief. The news of Pym's death had been long eagerly expected there, and when it arrived bonfires were lighted, and there was high carousing

among the Cavaliers. He was gone, the man
most needful to the commonwealth, and as it
seemed at the hour of her utmost need. But
before he went he had turned the tide, and
he bequeathed victory to his cause.

Had Pym lived and remained master of the
movement, what would have been the result?
Into what port did he mean to steer his revolution? To have embarked on the sea of civil
war without a port in view would not have
been the part of a great man. The indica-
tions are very slight in themselves; but taken
with the circumstances and the reason of the
case, they may perhaps amount to probability.
If my surmise is right, Pym would have preserved the monarchy, he would not have changed
the family, but he would have changed the
king. He would have put the king's nephew,
Prince Charles Louis, the eldest son of the Protestant heroine, Elizabeth Queen of Bohemia,
on the English throne. The prince, unlike his
brothers Rupert and Maurice, had shown sympathy with the Commons, and he was received
at London with much state just about the time
when Pym died. English history presented to
Pym's historic mind more than one example of

such a change of king. Thus he would have done in 1643 what was afterwards done in 1688, but he would probably have done it with a stronger and more statesmanlike hand, less in the interest of the aristocracy and the hierarchy, and more in the interest of the nation.

At the Restoration, Pym's body was torn, under a royal warrant, from its tomb, and thrown with the bodies of other rebels below the rank of regicide into a pit in the adjoining churchyard. The great man of the heroic age lies not beside the parliamentary tacticians whom our age calls great. As you stand on the north side of the nave of St. Margaret's Church, where some canons' houses once were, your feet are on the dust of Pym, of Blake and Dean, of Strode, of May the parliamentary historian, of Twiss the Prolocutor of the Assembly of Divines, of Dorislaus the martyred envoy of the Commonwealth, of Cromwell's mother, whom also the chivalry and piety of the Restoration tore out of her grave. Hampden had fallen and been buried in his own county, or his dust too would be there. In the vestibule of that vast and sumptuous but feebly conceived and effeminately ornamented pile, no unmeet shrine of Plutocracy, the present House of Commons, stand on either hand the statues of parliamentary worthies. Pym is not there. Ignorance probably it is that has excluded the foremost worthy of them all. Pym does not look down on the men who now fill the house which once he led; nor do they read on the pedestal of his statue the moral of his political life—" The best form of government is that which doth actuate and dispose every part and member of a state to the common good." But Pym has a statue in history, and seldom has there been more need for unveiling it than now.

CROMWELL.

II.

CROMWELL.

I HAVE called my subject "Cromwell." I ought, perhaps, rather to have called it the Protectorate. For to that part of Cromwell's life what I have to say will be almost entirely confined. I speak of him not as a general, or as a party leader, but as a prince.

In the early debates on religion, amidst the great orators of the Parliaments of Charles, there had stood up a gentleman farmer of Huntingdonshire, a fervent Puritan, with power on his brow and in his frame, with enthusiasm, genius, even the tenderness of genius in his eye; but in a dress which scandalised young courtiers, and with an unmusical voice, his sentences confused, his utterance almost choked by the vehemence of his emotion. On him God had not bestowed the gift of soul-enthralling words; his eloquence was the thunder of victory.

Victory went with him where he fought, when she had deserted the standards of all the other chiefs of his party. Hope shone in him " as a pillar of fire," when her light had gone out in all other men. He came to the front rank from the moment when debating was over, and the time arrived for organising war. From the first he rightly conceived the condition of success—a soldiery of yeomen fearing God, fearing nothing else, submitting themselves for the sake of their cause to a rigid discipline, as the only match for the impetuous chivalry of the Cavaliers : and his conception was embodied in the Ironsides. Marston crowns the first period of his career. It was won by the discipline of his men. Then came the struggle between his party, who wished to conquer, and the Presbyterians, who but half wished to conquer, who by this time hated the sectaries in their own ranks more than the common enemy, and whose aristocratic leaders now saw plainly that the revolution was going beyond the objects of an aristocracy, and that it was likely to do too much for the people. The Self-denying Ordinance set aside the Presbyterian commanders. It included in its

operation Cromwell. But Fairfax desired him,
before he resigned his command, to perform one
service more ; and it was felt, as it could not
fail to be felt, that to part with him was to
part with victory. This, as far as I can see,
not any intrigue of his, is the true account of
his retention in command. Naseby was won by
him with his new model army ; it made him
the first man in England ; though since Marston the adverse factions had been viewing his
rising greatness with a jealous eye, and vainly
plotting his overthrow. Then came the cap-
tivity and the death of the king, with the
interlude of Hamilton's Scotch invasion, and
the victory of Preston, gained in Cromwell's
fashion, which was not to manœuvre, but to
train his men well, march straight to his enemy,
and fight a decisive battle—a fashion natural
perhaps to one who had not studied the science
of strategy, but at the same time merciful, since
no brave men perished otherwise than in fight,
the loss of life was comparatively small, the results immense. Cromwell is now the general
of the Commonwealth : he conquers Ireland ;
he conquers Scotland ; the " crowning mercy "
of Worcester puts supreme power within his

grasp. After a pause, he makes himself Protector.

There are two points, dark spots as I think
them, in his career on which I must dwell to
pay a tribute to morality. The execution of
the King is treated by cynical philosophy in
its usual strain : " This action of the English
regicides did in effect strike a damp like death
through the heart of flunkeyism universally in
this world ; whereof flunkeyism, cant, cloth-
worship, and whatever other ugly name it
have, has gone about incurably sick ever since,
and is now at length in these generations very
rapidly dying." This is not the tone in which
the terrible but high-souled fanatics who did
it would have spoken of their own deed. They
at least so far respected the feelings of mankind, or rather their own feelings, as to drape
the scaffold with black. Cromwell would have
saved the king ; he would probably have made
terms with him, and, if he could have trusted
him, set him again upon his throne. Himself
a most tender husband and father, he had seen
Charles amidst his family, and had been touched.
But Charles could not see that he was fallen ;
his anointed kingship was still fact-proof. He

tried to play off one of the two contending
parties against the other when it was a matter
of life and death to them both. Cromwell discovered his duplicity. He then tried to frighten
Charles out of the kingdom, by sending him an
intimation at Hampton Court that there were
designs against his life. Charles fled from
Hampton Court, but, his flight being mis-
managed, he became a prisoner in the Isle of
Wight. There he negociated with the Parliament, in which the enemies of Cromwell and
the Independents were still strong. At the
same time he was carrying on the intrigues
with the Royalist faction which produced the
rising in Kent and the invasion of England by
Hamilton. Before the army marched against
Hamilton, the officers, exasperated at having
their lives and their cause thus again put in
peril, after so many bloody fields, by the
duplicity of the king, held a prayer meeting
at Windsor, and there resolved—" That it was
their duty, if ever the Lord brought them back
in peace, to call Charles Stuart, that man of
blood, to an account for the blood he had shed
and the mischief he had done to his utmost
against the Lord's cause and people in these

poor nations." They had before them a precedent in the case of Mary Stuart. When
they returned victorious, they signed a petition
" for justice and a settlement of the kingdom."
Cromwell sends the petition to Fairfax, with
a letter, saying, that he finds among the officers
of his regiment a great sense of the sufferings
of the kingdom, and a great zeal to have impartial justice done upon offenders. He adds
that he does himself from his heart concur with
them, and believes that God has put these things
into their hearts. Thus the king was brought
to trial and to the scaffold. This, so far as I can
see, is the real account of Charles's death, and
of Cromwell's share in it. Of Cromwell's own,
there is, touching this the gravest and most
questionable act of his life, no recorded word.
He does not touch on it in his speeches or his
letters; he appears not to have touched on it
in conversation with his friends. Never did a
man more completely carry his secret with him
to the grave. That the execution of the king
was a fatal error of policy is a thing so clear
to us, that we can scarcely suppose one so
sagacious as Cromwell to have been altogether
blind to it; and it is, therefore, reasonable to

suppose that his course was determined not by policy, but by sympathy with the feelings of his soldiers. The fierce and hard Old Testament sentiments which were in their hearts were in his heart too. Nothing, unhappily, can be less true than that the act of the regicides struck a damp through the heart of flunkeyism, or that flunkeyism has gone about incurably sick of it ever since. It is liberty, if anything, that has gone about sick of it. The blood of the royal martyr has been the seed of flunkeyism from that day to this. What man, what woman, feels any sentimental attachment to the memory of James II. ? There would have been less attachment, if possible, to the memory of the weak and perfidious Charles, if his weakness and his perfidy had not been glorified by his death.

The other point is the slaughter of the garrisons of Drogheda and Wexford. Here again the cynical philosophy, which from a satiety as it seems of civilisation we are beginning to affect, exults in the blow dealt to what it calls false philanthropy, rose-water, universal pardon and benevolence. It is to be hoped that these philosophers will, as soon as possible, tell us what philanthropy is not false, lest we should all become brutes together. The war in Ireland had been on both sides a war of extermination. The Catholics had begun it by a great massacre of the Protestants, on the reality or the atrocity of which it seems to me idle to cast a doubt, though assuredly if such deeds could ever be pardoned, they might be pardoned in a people so deeply wronged, so brutalised by oppression, as the Catholics of Ireland then were. These very garrisons had taken part, or were believed to have taken part, in cruelties worse than those committed by Nana Sahib. The feeling of English Protestants against the Papist rebels of Ireland, which of course Cromwell could not help sharing, was at least as strong as that of Englishmen in our own time against the Indian mutineers. Cromwell summoned both places to surrender, with an implied offer of mercy, before he stormed. The laws of war in those days were far less humane and chivalrous than they are now : the garrison of a place taken by storm was not held to have a right to quarter. The Catholic hero, Count Tilly, had put not only the garrison but the inhabitants of the great Protestant city of Magdeburg to the sword ; and the same thing had been done by Alva and other generals on the Catholic side. Cromwell says in his despatch : " I am persuaded that this is a righteous judgment of God upon these wretches, who have imbrued their hands in .so much innocent blood ; and that it will tend to prevent the effusion of blood for the future, which are the satisfactory grounds to such actions, which otherwise cannot but work remorse and regret." This excuse is not sufficient, if any innocent persons were involved in the slaughter ; no excuse can be sufficient for the shedding of innocent blood on any occasion or under any pretence, except in fair battle. But it is at all events the excuse of a moral and reasonable being. "Durst thou wed the heaven's lightning and say to it, Godlike one ?" This, I think, is the excuse of one who, under the influence of a literary theory, has for the moment divested himself of his morality and of his reason too.

We pass on then to the Protectorate. Great questions concerning both the Church and the State are still open; and till they are settled the judgment of history on Cromwell can scarcely be fixed. To some the mention of his reign still

recalls a transient domination of the powers of
evil breaking through the divine order of the
political and ecclesiastical world. Others regard
his policy as a tidal wave, marking the line to
which the waters will once more advance, and
look upon him as a ruler who was before his
hour, and whose hour perhaps is now come.
Here we must take for granted the goodness
of his cause, and ask only whether he served
it faithfully and well.

Of his genius there is little question. Clarendon himself could not be blind to the fact
that such a presence as that of this Puritan
soldier had seldom been felt upon the scene of
history. Necessity, "who will have the man
and not the shadow," had chosen him from
among his fellows and placed her crown upon
his brow. I say again let us never glorify revolution; let us not love the earthquake and
the storm more than the regular and beneficent
course of nature. Yet revolutions send capacity
to the front with volcanic force across all the
obstacles of envy and of class. It was long
before law-loving England could forgive one
who seemed to have set his foot on law; but
there never perhaps was a time when she was

not at heart proud of his glory, when she did not feel safer beneath the ægis of his victorious name. As often as danger threatens us, the thought returns, not that we may have again a Marlborough or a Black Prince ; but that the race which produced Cromwell may, at its need, produce his peer, and that the spirit of the Great Usurper may once more stand forth in arms.

Of Cromwell's honesty there is more doubt. And who can hope, in so complex a character, to distinguish accurately the impulses of ambition from those of devotion to a cause ? Who can hope, across two centuries, to pierce the secret of so deep a heart ? We must not trust the envious suggestions of such observers as Ludlow or even Whitelocke. Suspicions of selfish ambition attend every rise, however honest, however inevitable, from obscurity to power. Through "a cloud not of war only but detraction rude," the "chief of men" had " ploughed his glorious way to peace and truth." These witnesses against him are not agreed among themselves. Ludlow is sure that Cromwell played the part of an arch-hypocrite in pressing Fairfax to command the army of Scotland ; but Mrs. Hutchinson is sure that though he was an arch-hypocrite on other occasions, on this he was sincere. After the death of the king, after the conquest of Ireland, when the summit of his ambition must have been full in his view, he married his eldest son Richard to the daughter of a private gentleman, bargaining anxiously though not covetously about the settlement, and caring, it seems, for nothing so much as that the family with which the connection was formed should be religious. Can Richard have been then, in his father's mind, heir to a crown ?

Cromwell was a fanatic, and all fanatics are morally the worse for their fanaticism : they set dogma above virtue, they take their own ends for God's ends, and their own enemies for His. But that this man's religion was sincere who can doubt ? It not only fills his most private letters, as well as his speeches and despatches, but it is the only clue to his life. For it, when past forty, happy in his family, well to do in the world, he turned out with his children and exposed his life to sword and bullet in obscure skirmishes as well as in glorious fields. On his deathbed his thoughts wandered not like those of Napoleon among the eddies of battle or in

the mazes of statecraft, but among the religious
questions of his youth. Constant hypocrisy
would have been fatal to his decision. The
double-minded man is unstable in all his ways.
This man was not unstable in any of his ways :
his course is as straight as that of a great force
of nature. There is something not only more
than animal, but more than natural in his
courage. If fanatics so often beat men of the
world in council, it is partly because they throw
the die of earthly destiny with a steady hand
as those whose great treasure is not here.

Walking amidst such perils, not of sword and
bullet only, but of envious factions and intriguing enemies on every side, it was impossible that Cromwell should not contract a wariness, and perhaps more than a wariness of step.
It was impossible that his character should not
in some measure reflect the darkness of his time.
In establishing his government he had to feel
his way, to sound men's dispositions, to con-
ciliate different interests ; and these are processes not favourable to simplicity of mind, still
less favourable to the appearance of it, yet compatible with general honesty of purpose. As to
what is called his hypocritical use of Scriptural

language, Scriptural language was his native tongue. In it he spoke to his wife and children, as well as to his armies and his Parliaments : it burst from his lips when he saw victory at Dunbar : it hovered on them in death, when policy, and almost consciousness, was gone.

He said that he would gladly have gone back to private life. It is incredible that he should have formed the design, perhaps not incredible that he should have felt the desire. Nature no doubt with high powers gives the wish to use them ; and it must be bitter for one who knows that he can do great things, to pass away before great things have been done. But when great things have been done for a great end on an illustrious scene, the victor of Naseby, Dunbar, and Worcester, the saviour of a nation's cause, may be ready to welcome the evening hour of memory and repose, especially if, like Cromwell, he has a heart full of affection and a happy home.

Of the religion of hero-worship I am no devotee. Great men are most precious gifts of Heaven, and unhappy is the nation which cannot produce them at its need. But their importance in history becomes less as civilisation goes on.

A Timour or an Attila towers unapproachably
above his horde : but in the last great struggle
which the world has seen, the Cromwell was not
a hero, but an intelligent and united nation.
And to whatever age they may belong, the
greatest, the most god-like of men, are men, not
gods. They are the offspring, though the highest offspring, of their age. They would be nothing without their fellow-men. Did Cromwell
escape the intoxication of power which has
turned the brains of other favourites of fortune,
and bear himself always as one who held the
government as a trust from God ? It was because he was one of a religious people. Did
he, amidst the temptations of arbitrary rule,
preserve his reverence for law, and his desire
to reign under it ? It was because he was one
of a law-loving people. Did he, in spite of
fearful provocation, show on the whole remarkable humanity ? It was because he was one of
a brave and humane people. A somewhat larger
share of the common qualities—this, and this
alone it was which, circumstances calling him to
a great trust, had raised him above his fellows.
The impulse which lent vigour and splendour
to his government came from a great movement,

not from a single man. The Protectorate with
its glories was not the conception of a lonely
intellect, but the revolutionary energy of a
mighty nation concentrated in a single chief.

I can never speak of Mr. Carlyle without
paying grateful homage to the genius which
produced the " French Revolution." That work
is his best, partly perhaps because it is free
from a hero. His " Cromwell" is hero-worship,
and therefore it is not true ; but like the alche-
mists who made real chemical discoveries while
they were in search of their visionary gold,
though he has failed to reveal a god, he has
not failed to help us in our study of the
character of a great man.

Carlyle prostrates morality before greatness.
His imitators prostrate it before mere force,
which is no more adorable than mere fraud,
the force of those who are physically weak.
We might as well bow down before the hundred-
handed idol of a Hindoo. To moral force we
may bow down : but moral force resides and can
reside in those only whose lives embody the
moral law. It is found in the highest degree
in those at whom hero-worship sneers. Hero-
worship sneers at Falkland : yet Falkland by

his purity and his moderation has touched and influenced the hearts of his countrymen for ever. We shall come to the vulgar worship of success, and be confounded with those who look upon misfortune as the judgment of Heaven upon the vanquished. " The judgment of Heaven was upon them, sir," said a Tory bishop, speaking of the regicides, to Quin ; " the judgment of Heaven was upon them—almost all of them came to violent ends." " So, my lord," replied Quin, " did almost all the Apostles." What makes us men, not brutes, if it is not that we reverence ourselves, and listen to the god in our own breasts, instead of blindly following the animal whom victory in a conflict of force has marked out as the leader of our herd ?

Neither force do I worship in Cromwell nor arbitrary power. Milton was no Imperialist, no admirer of the Cæsars, no apologist of Nero. I hope to show some ground for thinking that arbitrary power was not dear to Cromwell's heart. He was great enough, if I mistake not, and felt himself great enough, to reign among the free. An ignoble nature like that of Bonaparte may covet despotism. A noble nature

never cared for the affection of a dependent
or for the obedience of a slave.

When a revolution is over, a government
must be founded, at once to gather in the fruits
and to heal the wounds of the struggle. And
the only men who can found it are those who
remain masters of the revolution. The man who
remained master of the English Revolution was
the victor of Worcester. The conquest of the
Royalists was not his only service, or his only
claim to supreme power. In the English, as
afterwards in the French Revolution, the foun-
tains of the social deep had at last been broken
up, and terrible forms of anarchy had begun to
appear. Cromwell had quelled anarchy as well
as tyranny. With a promptness and an integrity
which go far towards proving his paramount
devotion to the public good, as well as with
a courage, moral and personal, which has never
been surpassed, and at the same time with a
merciful economy of punishment which shows
how different is the vigour of the brave from
the vigour of the savage, he had confronted and
put down the great mutiny of the Levellers.
He had thus perhaps saved England from a
reign of terror. And they were no Parisian

street mob, these insurgents with whom he had
to deal, nor were their leaders the declaimers of
the Jacobin Club. They were the best soldiers
that ever trod a field of battle, the soldiers who
had gained his own victories, led by men of
desperate courage, and fighting for a cause in
which they were reckless of their lives.

The decimated remnant of the Long Parliament was not a government. It was a Revolutionary Assembly. It had lost the character of
a government when it deposed and beheaded
the king who had called it ; when it abolished
the other house, which was as essential a part
of a legal parliament as itself ; when it was
reduced to a fourth of its legal number by
Pride's Purge and other violent acts of the
revolution. Nor was it fit to become the government, though this was its aim. Revolutionary assemblies, while the struggle lasts and
egotism is subdued by danger, often display
not only courage, energy, and constancy, but
remarkable self-control. So sometimes do revolutionary mobs. But the struggle over, the
tendencies to faction, intrigue, tyranny, and
corruption begin to appear. The services of
the Long Parliament as a Revolutionary As-

sembly had been immense ; its name will be
held in honour while English liberty endures.
But when it was victorious and aspired to be
the government, its rule was the tyranny of a
section, insufferable to the great body of the
nation. It was a dominant faction, maintaining
itself in power by daily violence, prolonging all
the evils and imperilling all the fruits of the
revolution. In finance it was subsisting by
revolutionary expedients, by the sale of public
property, and what was much worse, by confiscation. Its office for sequestration in Haber-
dasher's Hall was crowded every day with the
trembling victims of its cruel deeds. It had
superseded the regular courts of justice by a
revolutionary tribunal which had put a man
to death for having acted as the emissary of
Charles II. at Constantinople. In foreign policy
it was running wild. It wanted to annex the
Dutch Republic, and when it was thwarted in
that chimerical scheme it plunged the two Protestant nations into a fratricidal and disastrous
war. That it showed in the conduct of that
war great Republican vigour, and by the hand
of Vane created a navy with marvellous ra-
pidity, was but a slight compensation for so

calamitous an error. The measure by which it was preparing to perpetuate its own existence was as much a usurpation as the assumption of supreme power by Cromwell. And yet what could it do without a permanent head of the state? Had it issued writs for a Free Parliament and dissolved, it would not only have committed suicide itself, but have plunged the nation into an abyss of anarchy and confusion.

Cromwell was set up by the army : whence an outcry against a government of musketeers and pikemen. A government of musketeers and pikemen is the greatest of calamities and the deepest of degradations ; and how to escape the danger of such government, which threatens all European nations in their critical transition from the feudal aristocracy of the past to the democracy of the future, is now a pressing question for us all. But the soldiers of Cromwell were not mere musketeers and pikemen. They were not like the legionaries of Cæsar and the grenadiers of Napoleon, raising the idol of the camp to a despotic throne. They were the best of English citizens in arms for the nation's cause ; and when all was over with the cause, they became the best of English citizens again.

Through them the Revolution had conquered ; they in truth were the Revolution. They had no right, and they had as little inclination, to set up a military tyranny ; but they had a right to give a chief to the State and to support the government of the chief whom they had given. It was in fact upon them and their general, not upon the nation or any considerable party in it, that the Parliament itself rested, and they and their general were accordingly responsible for its acts and for the continuance of its power.

Nor was the chief whom they gave to the nation a Cæsar ; much less was he a Bonaparte, an unprincipled soldier of fortune vaulting on the back of a Revolution to make himself an emperor. The relation of Cromwell to the English Revolution was not that of a Napoleon, but, if it is not blasphemy to mention the two names together, that of a Robespierre. The chief of the Rousseauists was the leader of the most religious and the deepest part of the French movement, though shallow was the deepest. Cromwell was in like manner himself the leader and embodiment of the most religious and the deepest part of the English movement. He was Puritanism armed and in power, not the suc-

cessful general of a foreign war. I say that in
the case alike of the English and of the French
Revolution the most religious part of the movement was the deepest part. The most religious
part of all movements is the deepest part. Beneath these social and political revolutions which
are now going on around us, and which seem to
move society so deeply, do ye not perceive,
deeper than all, a revolution in religion—a
revolution which may one day clothe itself in
some form of power and cast the world again
in a new mould ?

The form of government which Cromwell
meant to found was a monarchy, with himself
as monarch. I do not doubt that this was his
design from the time when he took supreme
power into his hands. But it was not to be
a Stuart monarchy. It was to be a Constitutional and a Protestant monarchy, with Parliamentary government, Parliamentary taxation,
reform of the representation, an enlightened
and vigorous administration, the service of the
State freely opened to merit, trial by jury, law
reform, church reform, university reform, the
union of the three kingdoms, a pacified and
civilised Ireland, and with no halting and

wavering foreign policy, but the glorious head-
ship of the Protestant cause in Europe; above
all with that to which Milton pointed as the
chief work of his chief of men, that for which
the leader of the Independents had throughout fought and suffered—liberty of conscience.
Cromwell might well think that he thus gave
the nation all the substantial objects for which
it had fought.   But how far in this policy personal ambition may have mingled with public
wisdom is a question which, as I said before, can
be answered by the Searcher of Hearts alone.

After the foundation of the monarchy would
necessarily have come a dynasty, with all the
accidents and infirmities to which dynasties
are liable; but this dynasty would have been
bound by stronger pledges than the Hanoverian
dynasty was to Protestantism and Constitutional
Government.

We need not sneer at the high aspirations of
Vane and the Republicans.   If some men did
not aspire too high, the world in general would
fall too low.   But few think that a democratic
republic would then have been possible even
for England; much less would it have been
possible for the three kingdoms, as yet most

imperfectly united, and two of them politically
in a very backward state. It must have been
an oligarchical republic like that of Holland:
and it must have been, for a long time at least,
a party republic. Vane said that none were
worthy to be citizens who had not fought for
liberty. There would thus have been no prospect of reconciliation or of oblivion: the fruit
of the nation's sufferings would have been a
chronic civil war. It was time to make England again a nation. This a national government alone could do. And as matters stood,
the government of a single chief, raised in some
measure above all parties, could alone be national. Cromwell's first act after Worcester
had been to press on the parliament a general
amnesty, in which he was supposed as usual
to have some sinister end in view. The first
day of his reign was the last of confiscation
and of vengeance. From that day every Ca-
valier was safe in person and estate; might,
after a short probation, regain the full rights
of a citizen; might, by mere submission to the
established government and without injury to
his honour, become eligible to the highest offices
of the state.

The conduct of Cromwell has been contrasted with that of Washington. The two cases were quite different. In the case of Washington there had not been a civil war in the proper sense of the term, but a national struggle against an external power, which left the nation united under a national government at its close. England, as Cromwell said in his rough way, stood in need of a constable : America did not.

On the other hand, the insulting violence of the manner in which Cromwell turned out the Long Parliament is not to be justified. That scene leaves a stain on his character as a man and as a statesman. By thus setting his heel on the honour of those with whom he had acted, and whose commission he bore, he was guilty of a breach of good policy as well as of right feeling. He needlessly stamped the origin of his own government with the character of violent usurpation, and he made for himself deadly enemies of all those on whom he had trampled. It is not improbable that he was hurried away by his emotions, which, dissembler as he is supposed to have been, sometimes got the better, to an extraordinary

extent, of his outward self-control: and that,
having wound himself up by a great effort to
a doubtful act, he went beyond his mark, and
launched out into language and gestures which
to those who witnessed them seemed insane.
In his first speech to the Little Parliament, he
paid at least a tribute of homage to legality
and right feeling. "I speak here in the presence of some that were at the closure of our
consultations, and as before the Lord — the
thinking of an act of violence was to us worse
than any battle than ever we were in, or that
could be, to the utmost hazard of our lives:
so willing were we, even very tender and desirous, if possible, that these men might quit
their places with honour." Be it remembered,
too, that there was no insolent parade of military power. Cromwell went down to the
house not in uniform, but in plain clothes.
Much less were there the arrests, the street
massacres, and the deportations, which constitute the glory of a *coup d'état* in France.

To restore the Constitutional and Protestant
monarchy in his own person was Cromwell's
aim. In this enterprise he had against him
all the parties; but he might flatter himself

that he had the secret wishes and the tendencies of the nation on his side. He had in his favour the divisions among his enemies, which were such that they could scarcely ever act in concert; his own surpassing genius; a temperament which never knew despair; a knowledge of men gained by reading the heart when it is most open, at the council-board in dangerous extremity, or on the eve of battle by the camp-fire side. And the army, though opposed in the main to his design of restoring the monarchy, was bound to his person by the spell of victory.

The step from civil war to legal government cannot be made at once. There must be a period of transition, during which government is half military, half legal, and while law is gradually resuming its sway, the efforts of the defeated parties to prevent a government from being founded will have to be repressed by force. It will be the duty of the head of the government to see that his measures of repression are strong enough and not too strong; that he hastens, as much as the enemies of the government will permit, the restoration of the reign of law. Cromwell well understood the true

doctrine of political necessity. " When matters
of necessity come," he said to his parliament,
" then without guilt extraordinary remedies
may be applied ; but if necessity be pretended,
there is so much the more sin." He did not
allow the government to be military for an
hour ; but at once summoning the Barbones
Parliament, rendered up his authority into their
hands. " To divest the sword of all power in
the civil administration" was the declared object of the great soldier in summoning this
assembly. A parliament the assembly is called ;
but it was not elective or representative ; it
was a convention of Puritan notables called by
Cromwell. It was denounced at the time and
has since been commonly regarded as a junta
of fanatics who wanted to sweep away law,
learning, and civil society to make room for the
code of Moses and the reign of the saints. It
went to work in eleven committees ; for the
reform of the law ; for the reform of prisons ;
for the reform of the finances and the light-
ening of taxation ; for Ireland ; for Scotland ;
for the army ; for petitions ; for public debts ;
for the regulation of the commissions of the
peace and the reform of the poor-law ; for the

advancement of trade ; for the advancement
of learning. Among its proceedings we find
measures for the care of lunatics and idiots,
for the regular performance of marriages and
the registration of births and deaths, for probate
of wills in all counties, for law reforms which
pointed both to a more speedy and cheaper
administration of justice and to the preparation
of a simple and intelligible code of law. We
have not yet carried into effect the whole pro-
gramme of these mad fanatics ; but we have
carried into effect a good part of it, and we
are hoping to carry into effect the rest. But
the Barbones Parliament was wanting in knowledge of government : it attempted too much
and it went too fast, common faults in a revolution, when the minds of men are stimulated to
the morbid activity of political thought. It
aroused the formidable opposition of all the
lawyers and of all the ministers of religion :
it showed an inclination prematurely to reduce
the army, which, it is idle to doubt, was still the
indispensable support not only of the general's
power, but of the Cause ; and, moreover, it did
not do the essential thing ; it did not take
measures for the foundation of a government,

while it had no title to be the government itself.
Cromwell determined to bring its sittings to an
end. As usual, it is thought that he was playing a deep game, that he had foreseen that the
Barbones Parliament must fail and that its
failure would render him more indispensable
than ever. A deep game indeed, to bring together the leading men among your own friends,
discredit them by failure, and then make them
your enemies by sending them away! If Cromwell intended that the Barbones Parliament
should prove a failure he took a strange way
to his end, for he undoubtedly summoned to it
the best men he could find—men so good that
his enemies were greatly chagrined at seeing an
assembly so respectable answer to his call. The
Machiavellian theory of his conduct was easily
framed after the event : no sagacity could have
framed it before.

Cromwell now called a council of leading men,
civilians as well as soldiers, to settle the government : and this council made him Lord Protector of the three kingdoms, with the provisional constitution called the Instrument of
Government. And if Cromwell set up arbitrary
power, here is the arbitrary power which he set

up. The executive government is to be vested
in an elective Protector and a Council of State.
The members of the Council of State for the
first turn are named in the Instrument. When
a vacancy occurs, Parliament is to elect six candidates; of these six the Council of State is to
choose two, and of these two the Protector is
to choose one. The powers of legislation and
taxation are to be vested in Parliament alone,
the Protector having only a suspensive veto for
twenty days. A Parliament is to be held once at
least in every three years. The Protector is to
have the disposal of the army with the consent
of the Parliament when Parliament is sitting,
of the elective Council of State when it is not.
In the event of war, Parliament is at once to be
convoked. The Protector and the Council are
empowered to frame ordinances for the government of the country till Parliament meets; a
temporary provision, which only gave a legal
character to an inevitable exercise of power. It
was probably designed by the chief framers of
the Instrument that the elective Protector should
make way for an hereditary king; but no design was ever entertained of departing from the
constitutional principles on which this settle-

ment was based : on the contrary, those principles were afterwards most distinctly ratified in the document called the Petition and Advice, under which Cromwell was invited to take upon him the title of king. The Protector declared himself content to submit to all these limitations of his power, and ready to submit to further limitations, if by so doing he could satisfy the Parliament and give peace to the nation.

The constitution enacted by the Instrument presents several points of interest. Government under it can hardly be party government, the members of the Council of State being elected by personal merit, for life, and under conditions which prevent the Council from becoming a cabinet or cabal. Provision is made for the permanent existence of a national council, even in the Parliamentary recess. The army is brought thoroughly under the constitution. The nation is secured against the danger of being entangled in a war, without its own consent, by the ministers of the crown. The organic legislation of Cromwell's time may still deserve the consideration of constitutional reformers, if the nation should ever desire to emancipate itself from the government of party, which by

its faction-fights, its rogueries, its hypocrisies, the ascendancy which it gives to mere Parliamentary gladiators,—if the name of gladiator is not profaned by applying it to the hero of a venomous tongue,—and by its failures at home and abroad, must be beginning to breed serious thoughts in the mind of every independent lover of his country.

The Instrument embodied a measure of Parliamentary Reform, which Clarendon says was fit to be more warrantably made and in a better time. The representation was fairly redistributed on the basis of population. The small boroughs were swept away. Representatives were given to large towns hitherto unrepresented, Manchester among the number. The county representation was greatly increased; Yorkshire, for example, having fourteen members. Not only real but personal property was admitted as a qualification for the county franchise, every person being empowered to vote who had property of any kind to the value of £200, so that the copyholders, of whom there were a large number at that period, would have been enfranchised, as well as the leaseholders for lives, who were also a numerous class. Tenants at will, on the other

hand, would not have been enfranchised unless they had independent property, to the requisite value, of their own. The result would have been most worthy and independent county constituencies, consisting in great measure of the yeomen, whose political virtue and military valour had just saved and still sustained the country. The borough franchise, with all its varieties of suffrage, was left untouched. If this measure still does not sound democratic, we must bear in mind that serfage had but recently ceased to exist in England, while its traces still lingered in Scotland ; that the manufacturing interest and the artisan class were in their infancy ; that this was the last stage of the feudal, whereas ours is the industrial era. To know the value of Cromwell's Reform, we have only to consider what the rotten boroughs, to which the Restoration of course reverted, did for us in the two centuries which followed the Protectorate.

The Protector was now installed with moderate state, and on the next 3rd of September, his lucky day, he took the first great step towards the restoration of Constitutional Government by meeting his first Parliament. That

Parliament proved refractory. Instead of voting the necessary supplies and doing the business of the country, its members fell to questioning the right of the Protector. The answer to their questionings was simple. If they wanted divine right, it was by the Protector's hand that God had saved them all. If they wanted human right, it was by virtue of his writ that they were there. In the end it was found necessary to put to each member a test, in the form of an engagement to be faithful to the established government by a single person and a parliament. The test was nothing more than was implied in the writ under which each member had been elected ; yet many of the Republicans refused it and were excluded. Even after this purging, the Parliament remained intractable. It spent its time in the persecution of a Socinian, and showed a tendency to tamper with the fundamental principle on which Cromwell always insisted—liberty of conscience. The Protector at last dissolved it, with thunder in his voice and on his brow ; and in doing so he did well.

He was now driven again to govern for a time without Parliament ; and the Royalist plots and risings obliged him to appoint major-generals. But his government was taking root. The nation felt the beneficence of his administration ; the glories of its foreign policy touched its heart. Men contrasted them with the ignominy of the Stuarts, as when the Stuarts were restored they had reason to do again. The tidings of Blake's victories were ringing through England when the Protector again met a Parliament.

This time nothing was to be risked. The known malcontents were from the first excluded. Their exclusion, though veiled under a legal form, was an act of arbitrary power. The justification for it was, that if these members had been allowed to take their seats, they would have done their best to overturn the government ; that, if they had overturned the government, they would have brought in not the Republic of which Vane dreamed, nor the Reign of the Saints of which Harrison dreamed, nor the Covenanted King and the Calvinistic Church of which the Presbyterians dreamed, but the Stuarts ; and that if they had brought in the Stuarts, they would have cancelled the revolution, wrecked the cause, and set their own heads on Temple Bar.

After the exclusion, the Parliament still numbered three hundred and sixty members, friendly in the main. And now the time was come for the great attempt. A long train of waggons bore through London streets the spoils and trophies of Blake's victories over Spain. A poet was writing—

> "Let the brave generals divide that bough,
>   Our great Protector hath such wreaths enow :
>   His conquering head has no more room for bays,
>   Then let it be as the glad nation prays;
>   Let the rich ore forthwith be melted down,
>   And the State fixed by making him a crown :
>   With ermine clad and purple let him hold
>   A royal sceptre made of Spanish gold."

By the series of resolutions called the Petition and Advice the Protector was invited to take upon him the government by a higher title, and with a second house, which was to consist of seventy members to be named by the chief magistrate with the consent of parliament. Then followed the most anxious deliberation in Cromwell's life. He spoke himself of royalty with indifference, as a feather in the cap, the shining bauble for crowds to kneel and gaze at. I am ready, for my part, to believe that a man who has done such things in such a cause may, by the grace of heaven, keep his heart above tinsel. But we know why the title of king might, apart from any love of tinsel, seem essential to his policy. The lawyers could not get on without it ; the people, as they then were, craved for it. It was constitutional, whereas that of Protector was not constitutional : it saved persons adhering to the king *de facto* under the statute of Henry VII., whereas that of Protector did not. But the stern Republicans of the army were resolute against monarchy. It was not for a king that they had shed their blood. To their opposition Cromwell for the present yielded. Probably he not only yielded to it, but respected it. To be turned from his course by fear, it has been truly said, was not a failing to which he was prone. But ardent, sanguine, inexhaustible in resources as he was, he was the victim of no illusions. He knew the difference between the difficult and the impossible ; he faced difficulty without fear, and he recognised impossibility without repining, and again turned his mind steadily towards the future.

So Cromwell mingled not with the crowd of kings. He wore no crown but " Worcester's laureat wreath," and the more laureat wreath of

Milton's verse. Fate ordained that he should stand in history a chief of the people.

Part of the Petition and Advice however was carried into effect. The Protectorate had been elective. The Protector was now empowered to name his successor. There had hitherto been only one House of Parliament : there were now to be two, and the still half-feudal instincts of the nation were to be indulged with a House of Lords. This was the first Parliamentary settlement of the new constitution ; the Instrument of Government under which the Protector had hitherto acted having been framed as a provisional arrangement by a council of military and political chiefs. To mark the legal commencement of his power the Protector was installed with more solemnity than before, and with ceremonies more resembling a coronation, the account of which is given us by Whitelocke, who, though no lover of Cromwell, seems to have been impressed with the scene. In Westminster Hall, under a canopy of state, was placed a chair of state upon an ascent of two degrees, with seats down the hall for the parliament, the dignitaries of the law, the mayor and aldermen of London. Thither on the 26th of June, 1657, went the Protector with his council of state, his ministers, his gentlemen, sergeants-at-arms, officers, and heralds. His Highness standing under the canopy of state, the Speaker, in the name of the Parliament, put on him a robe of purple velvet lined with ermine, delivered to him the Bible, richly gilt and bossed, girt on him the sword of state, and put a golden sceptre into his hand. The same functionary then gave him the oath to observe the constitution, with solemn good wishes for the prosperity of his government. Mr. Manton, the chaplain, next by prayer recommended the Protector, the parliament, the council, the forces by land and sea, the whole government and people of the three nations to the blessing and protection of God. Then the people gave a shout and the trumpets sounded. The Protector took his seat in the chair of state, with the ambassadors of the friendly nations and the high officers of the Protectorate round him ; and as he did so the trumpets sounded again, heralds proclaimed the title of his Highness, and the people shouted once more " God save the Lord Protector." So looked sovereignty when for a moment it emerged from feudalism and showed

itself in the aspect of the modern time. At
the gorgeous coronation of Napoleon, some one
asked the Republican General Augereau whether
anything was wanting to the splendour of the
scene? "Nothing," replied Augereau, "but the
presence of the million of men who have died
to do away with all this." There was not much
in Cromwell's installation to do away with which
any man of sense had died. We got back afterwards to the more august and venerable cere-
mony, with the bishops, the anointings, the
champion in armour, and the glorious expense,
which the finances of the Protectorate could ill
bear. At the coronation of George III., as
Horace Walpole tells us, Lord Talbot, the Lord
Steward, had taught his horse to back all down
the hall after his rider had delivered the cup to
the king; but the too-well-trained animal insisted on backing into the hall and going all
up it with its tail in the king's face.

The second Parliament wasted time and violated the Protector's principles by the persecution of Naylor, a poor victim of the religious
frenzy which had seized many weak natures
in the vortex of a religious revolution. But it
voted supplies, and on the whole acted cordially

with the Protector. Hope dawned on the grand
enterprise.

Its dawn was again overcast. When Parliament met after the recess, it was with the
excluded members restored to their seats, and
with an Upper House. The Upper House was
a failure. An old aristocracy may be patched
to any extent, especially if some freedom is
allowed in constructing Norman pedigrees; but
to make a new one when the age of conquest
and conquering races is past, is happily not
an easy thing. Cromwell got few men of territorial or social consequence to sit, and he
incurred many damaging refusals. He said
that he wanted something to stand between
him and the Lower House, his direct contests
with which were no doubt bringing a heavy
strain upon his government. But to make up
his House of Lords, he had to take many of
his supporters from the Lower House, where
the great battle of supplies was to be fought,
and probably to break up the lead for the
government there. The result was that the
Lower House fell foul of the Upper, and
the ship became unmanageable once more. At
the same time, and perhaps in consequence of·

the distress of the Government, conspiracies, both Royalist and Republican, had broken out on the most formidable scale. It was necessary at once to dismiss Parliament, and to deal with this danger. And so effectually was it dealt with, though at a small cost of blood, that, after this, the Royalists rose no more. The hopes of that party, in the eyes of the shrewdest judges in Europe, were dead : and Charles Stuart could scarcely obtain common courtesy, much less recognition or support, from Mazarin or Don Louis de Haro. Only the Presbyterians had the power which, when Cromwell was gone, they used with such happy results to the nation and themselves, of setting the Stuarts again upon the throne.

In these contests with refractory parliaments, the great soldier and statesman had to play the part of an orator. He was too old to learn a new art. He did not prepare his speeches ; and when he was asked to write down one of them a few days after it had been delivered, he declared that he could not remember a word of it. Clumsier or more uncouth compositions than the reports which have come down to us, the records of bad oratory do not contain. The

grammar is hopeless, the metaphors and con-
fusions of metaphor most grotesque — " God
kindling a seed"—" the Lord pouring the nation
from vessel to vessel, till He poured it into your
lap." The last editor only makes the matter
worse by his running commentary of admiring
ejaculations. But the speeches are not kings'
speeches. There runs through them all a strong
though turbid tide of thought. They are the
utterances of one who sees his object clearly,
presses towards it earnestly, and struggles to
bear forward in the same course the reluctant
wills and wavering intellects of other men. The
great features of his situation, the great principles on which he was acting, are brought out,
as M. Guizot says, with a breadth and force,
which are a strong proof of a statesmanlike
intellect, and not a small proof perhaps of good
faith. But he pleaded to deaf ears. It is vain
to rail at those who refused to listen to him,
and who thwarted him to the end. They were
not great men. They were contending, many
of them at least, in singleness of heart, for what
they believed to be the good cause. They might
say with truth that Cromwell had changed ;
that the language of the Revolutionary Soldier

was not that of the Head of the State ; that his mind had grown more comprehensive, his vision clearer since he had risen to a higher point of view and into serener air : and, as he had changed, they might represent him to themselves as a renegade and a traitor. These misunderstandings between men who yesterday stood side by side are another mournful part of revolutions. We owe those who resisted Cromwell forbearance and respect. So far as they were struggling for English law against what they believed to be lawless power, we owe them gratitude. Principles are worth incomparably more than any possible benefits of any one man's rule. Yet the conduct of these patriots brought ruin on all they loved.

When Parliament refused the necessary supplies, the Protector was compelled to levy the old taxes by an ordinance in Council : but he did this with manifest reluctance, and with a manifest desire to return to Parliamentary taxation, as well as to Parliamentary government in other respects. The spoils of the Spanish galleons helped his finances for a time. A less noble source of supply was an income-tax of ten per cent. levied on the Royalists after their great

revolt. In that great resource, frugality, the
government of Cromwell was rich; considering
what it did, it was the cheapest government
England ever had. But the truth is, greatness
is generally cheap: it is littleness aping greatness that is so dear. The Protector offered to
lay the financial administration open to the most
rigorous inspection. He was not afraid, he said,
on that score to face the nation. He was ready,
in fact, to do anything, except to allow the
government to be overturned : rather than that,
he said, he would be rolled with infamy into his
grave.

All this time he had been struggling with a
series of plots against his power and his life.
The ground on which his tottering throne was
reared heaved on all sides with conspiracy and
rebellion. The plotters were not only Royalists
but fanatical Republicans, leaguing themselves
in their frenzy with Royalists to their own
destruction. To the Republicans Cromwell behaved as to old friends estranged. The utmost
that he did was to put them for a time in
safe keeping, when they would have laid desperate hands on the life of their own cause. He
was careful too of their honour ; and so long as

they would be quiet, never put to them any
oath or test. With the Royalists he dealt rigorously, as old enemies, yet mercifully, as all fear-
less natures do. When they had risen in arms
against him, he placed them under the control
of the Major-Generals, and laid on them, not
a fine of the tenth part of their property, but an
income-tax of ten per cent. It is said that this
taxing of the Royalists was a breach of the Act
of Oblivion. It was so ; but what was their
insurrection ?

In the punishment of political offences, Cromwell did his best to return from the revolutionary high courts of justice to trial by jury.
The first case with which he had to deal was
that of Lilburn, an aimless and egotistical agi-
tator, though otherwise pure and brave, who
had returned from exile merely to prevent the
settlement of the nation. Lilburn was sent
before a jury; but the jury being strong par-
tisans, and the court being crowded with the
friends of the accused, the government failed
to obtain a conviction, and was driven to the
worst course of all—that of mixing force
with law, by keeping Lilburn in custody after
his acquittal. The conspirators in Vowell and

Gerrard's plot, and those in Slingsby's plot, were sent before a high court of justice. But Cromwell's high court of justice was not like the French revolutionary tribunal, or an Irish or Jamaica court-martial. It consisted of a large number of judges, including the highest functionaries of the law, it sat publicly, proceeded deliberately, and observed the legal rules of evidence : nor, unless to murder the Protector and overturn the government was no offence, does the slightest suspicion rest upon it of having shed one drop of innocent blood. The Royalists taken in Penruddock's rebellion were tried before juries in the counties where the rebellion occurred : so little known to this military despot were our present theories of martial law. The daggers of the Royalists were always threatening the Protector's life. And not their daggers only : a proclamation was circulated, in the name of the exiled king, promising great rewards and honours to whoever would take the usurper off with pistol, sword, or poison. It is commonly believed that his nerves were completely shaken by the fear of assassination; but the well-known passage of Hume, describing the Protector's agonies of alarm, is a rhetorical improvement on the passage in the rabidly Royalist work of Dr. Bates, the court physician to Charles II., and I believe the statement has no trustworthy foundation. Cromwell, of course, took the necessary precautions, and as the author of "Killing no Murder" assured him, great precautions were necessary; but there is nothing in his bearing or in his policy to the end of his life to show that fear had shaken his fortitude; and assuredly it did not shake his clemency. Of the forty men arrested for Vowell and Gerrard's plot, three only were sent before the high court of justice, and of those three one was spared. In Slingsby's plot five persons only suffered, though it was a formidable conspiracy, to deliver Hull to the Spaniards, and at the same time to raise an insurrection in London, which would have filled the city with fire and blood. Few besides the actual leaders suffered death for Penruddock's rebellion, though a good many of their followers were transported. Fear for his government, though his life was in no danger, impelled Bonaparte to murder a Bourbon prince who had approached his frontier. Ormond, Cromwell's most formidable, as well

as his most honourable enemy, came to London
in disguise to get up a plot against the government. His presence was detected. Cromwell took Lord Broghil, Ormond's former associate, aside, and said to him, "If you wish to
do a kindness to an old friend, Ormond is in
London; warn him to begone." Those were
harder times than ours, and civil war begets
recklessness of human life: but the strongest
man of those times in his true strength has
bequeathed a lesson to the emasculate sen-
timentalism which counterfeits manliness by
affecting sympathy with deeds of violence and
blood.

There can be no doubt that the Stuart
princes and their advisers were privy to assassination plots. Cromwell had threatened
that if they used assassins, he would make it a
war of assassination. But he was not a Stuart
prince, and he never degraded his nobler nature
by putting his threat in execution.

Algernon Sidney, staunch republican as he
was, told Burnet that the Protector had just
notions of public liberty. In one respect at
least he had juster notions of liberty than his
parliaments, for he stood out against them for

freedom of conscience, and his veto on acts of persecution was one of the powers which he would never let go. "To save free conscience" was the special task to which he had been called by one who understood the interests of freedom of conscience well, and he seems to have performed that work faithfully according to his lights, which it is especially necessary, with reference to this subject, to bear in mind were not those of an inspired hero, but those of an uninspired Puritan of the seventeenth century, sitting at the feet of Hugh Peters and in thraldom to Hugh Peters's superstitions, believing in the necessity of dogma, and believing, we may be quite sure, in witchcraft. Theoretically, of course, his toleration embraced only Protestants and Trinitarians, all sects of whom he desired to see not only at peace with each other, but united, in spite of those secondary differences which he deemed of no importance compared with the vital principles of the Christian faith. But the greatness of his nature carried him beyond his theory, and in all cases we find him practically the enemy of persecution. He snatched Biddle, the Socinian, from the fangs of Parliament, placed him in mild confinement, and, so soon as it was safe, set him free. He tried to procure the formal readmission of the Jews to England, from which they had been banished since the time of Edward I., and, failing in this, he protected individual Jews who settled in this country. He left the Roman Catholics practically unmolested in conscience and in their private worship, while they were burning Protestants alive wherever they had the power, though he could not have permitted the open celebration of the mass without causing an outbreak among the people. The persecution of Catholic priests, which had been going on during the latter days of the Parliament, soon abated when he became Protector. At one time he launched some fierce ordinances both against the Catholics and the Anglicans, not on account of their religious opinions but on account of their political plots and insurrections. Generally the Anglicans enjoyed under him as much liberty as they could expect, when the foot of Laud had but just been taken from the neck of the nation. All sects, in fact, even the most unpopular, even those which the Protector himself most hated and had the

bitterest reason to hate as the nurseries not only
of his political opponents but of the assassins
who sought his life, provided they would only
abstain from active attempts to overthrow the
government, were sure of obtaining under that
government the utmost measure of freedom
which could be expected from the most liberal
spirit of that age.   The Presbyterians, who had
persecuted Cromwell with the most unrelenting
malignity, were never persecuted by him.   On
the contrary, his scheme of church polity comprehended them, and he was most desirous that
they should come in.   It was in this matter of
freedom of conscience that the man was most
before his age, and that the most momentous
issues hung upon his life : issues how momentous we see from the religious perplexity
and distress into which, partly by the reversal
of his policy, we have been brought.   Reasons
have been already given for believing that this
was in him, not the toleration of indifference,
but the real toleration of a man of strong conviction.   Much as his mind had grown in
stature, he remained to the last open to the
impressions even of very fanatical preachers
of the doctrines which had been the spring of

his own spiritual life. He liked to commune
with such enthusiasts as Foxe. This may have
been, and no doubt was, partly policy: it was
to persecuted sectaries that the government of
the Independent chief especially appealed. But
great simplicity of religious feeling is compatible
with high intellect: and, after all, the enthusiasts, who, whenever the spirit of the world
is deeply moved, come forth preaching a more
equal state of society, and a brotherhood of
man, are they the people whom the profoundest
political philosophy would most despise? Are
they mere dreamers, or do they dream of that
which is to come?

When we consider that the Protector's reign
lasted but five years and that it was a constant
struggle for the existence of his government
and his own life, and when we think what he
achieved, we must allow that his administration
was as high a proof of practical capacity as was
ever given by man. Or rather, it was as high
a proof as ever was given of the power of a
nation when, in a moment of extraordinary
exaltation, the nation finds a worthy organ in
its chief.

In the department of justice, the Protector

put upon the bench the best judges probably that England had ever had, and at their head Sir Matthew Hale. He made strenuous efforts to reform those monstrous delays and abuses of the Court of Chancery, which afterwards insulted reason and sullied public justice for nearly two hundred years. He wished to reform the criminal law, which the Tudor despots and their aristocratic parliaments had made a code of blood. " It was a scandalous thing," he said, " that a man should be hanged for a theft of twelvepence or sixpence when greater crimes went unpunished." A man of the people, he did not share the aristocratic recklessness of plebeian blood, which had lavished, and which when he was gone lavished still more, capital punishment for vulgar offences, while the worse offences of the privileged class went free. Had he succeeded, the work of Romilly would have been performed, in part at least, two centuries before.

Everything was done to foster commerce, and that interest seems at this time to have received a permanent impulse, which bore it prosperously onwards even through the maladministration and the naval disasters of the Restoration. A

Committee of Trade was formed, and White-locke, who was one of its members, says that this was an object on which the Protector's heart was greatly set. Other than territorial interests were now held to deserve care. If on the subject of navigation laws Cromwell was a Protectionist, so on the same subject was Adam Smith. Slowly the light dawns even on the highest peaks of thought.

A navy had been created by the Parliament in the war with the Dutch ; when Vane, at the head of the Admiralty, had shown that energy, purity, and public spirit, added to intellect, will make a great administrator, even of a man who has not passed his life in office. But the Pro-tector fostered that navy so well that if Blake is the father of our naval tactics, Cromwell is the father of our naval greatness.

The army, which found no equal in the field, and on whose invincible prowess Clarendon could not help dilating when it was disbanded by Charles II., was in discipline equally without a peer. Though the Protector's power rested on the soldiery, their licence, if ever it broke out, was rigorously repressed. In this so-called military government, no soldier was above the law. The swaggering truculence of the prætorian towards fellow-citizens has no connection with the military qualities which are the pledges of victory over the enemy in the field.

Among the Chancellors of the University of Oxford, the name of Oliver stands a startling reality in a line of stately buckram. Cromwell was not, like Pym and Hampden, highly cultivated ; but he had been bred at a classical school and at Cambridge ; and, what was of more consequence, he had been trained intellectually by converse with the highest intellects on the highest subjects of the time. No brutal soldier, no drill-sergeant, was he ; nor does his policy as a democratic chief afford any reason for believing that democracy will be the enemy of culture. Though unlearned himself, he fostered learning ; he saved and protected the Universities of Oxford and Cambridge. He founded the University of Durham. Learned men and men of intellect of the opinions most opposed to his own, studied and wrote in security beneath his rule. Turn where you will, you find him, when he is left to himself, sympathising with what is noble, and a magnanimous friend to freedom. Alone of English princes, he set himself to draw merit and promise from the Universities into the service of the State. The men whom he placed at the head of Oxford were Puritans of course, but they were learned men and ruled well; and the University improved in nothing, except in political and religious principles, when they were gone.

Cromwell's church reform, as well as his university reform, was Puritan, but it was comprehensive. It was directed more to piety than doctrine, and it imposed no tests. It left an Established Church; but it enlarged the liberties of that Church to the utmost extent possible to the reformer, or even conceivable by his mind; and aimed at making the Establishment national by taking in the whole nation, not by crushing the nation into a sect. It gave the people good ministers. Not only was it the most liberal settlement of its time, but nothing so liberal followed for ages afterwards. Baxter, who was no friend of Cromwell's, allows that the Protector's commissioners "put in able and serious preachers, who lived a godly life, of what tolerable opinion soever they were, so that many thousands of souls blessed God." And thus the people gained that for which Cromwell himself had taken arms, and which in his eyes was the great object of the civil war.

The conquest of Scotland was followed by an incorporating union. Thus was achieved what, down to that time, had been the greatest object of English policy. Representatives of Scotland were called to the Protector's Parliaments. The country was necessarily occupied for some time by an army : but that army did not insult or oppress the people. As Independents, no doubt they paid scanty respect to the divine right of the Kirk. They sometimes took the word of God out of His minister's mouth, and sat in derision on the stool of repentance. In a few cases, it is to be feared, they guided Scottish maidens in paths which did not lead to heaven. But their conduct generally seems to have been better than that of any other soldiers in a conquered country. So far is religious fanaticism from being the root of all vice in man. The heritable jurisdictions, with their oppressive absurdities, were swept away, and Scotch law courts, the greatest nests of corruption in the legal world, saw for a time the unwonted face of justice. " Deil think them, a ween kinless loons," was the pensive reflection of an old

Scotch jobber. These were fine days everywhere for kinless loons. "We count those
years," says Burnet, "years of great prosperity."
The patriot statesmen of the Restoration dissolved the Union, and undid the Protector's
work, that they might exercise in Scotland a
provincial despotism, unchecked even by a Parliament of Cavaliers.

The Irish talk of the curse of Cromwell.
They ought rather to talk of the curse of the
Cromwellians. The real oppressors were the
military adventurers and the State creditors,
to whom the Long Parliament had assigned as
payment the confiscated lands of the Irish land-
owners implicated in the rebellion. That Cromwell intended to exterminate the Irish is an
exploded fable : from the moment when the
rebellion was suppressed, he bade the mass of
the Irish people dwell in security and peace.
His rule unhappily was that of a Puritan over
Papists, of an Anglo-Saxon conqueror over conquered Celts, and this in an age when the
highest minds were almost inevitably victims
to prejudices of religion and race of which the
lowest minds ought now to be ashamed ; but
still it was the best government that Ireland

had ever had. By uniting Ireland to England and calling her representatives to his parliaments he brought her under imperial rule, the surest protection against local tyranny that he could give. His policy in this respect was ratified after another century and half of disunion and ascendancy by Pitt, or rather by those calamities which great men avert, but which to ordinary men are the only teachers of wisdom. The chiefs of the Irish government and law were appointed, not by a Dublin faction, but by him. He sent over an excellent viceroy in the person of his son Henry, to whom he gave counsels of gentleness and moderation; and with complaints of the wrongs done to the Irish people we find mingled the mention of the Protector's name as that of a power (though, no doubt, he was too distant a power) of justice. He even saw with a statesman's eye what Ireland from its very backwardness and unsettlement might be made to do for England. In a conversation with Ludlow, after dwelling on the delays and expensiveness of English law, he added that Cooke, the Chief Justice whom he had sent to Ireland, determined more causes in a week than Westminster Hall in a year.

" Ireland," he went on to say, " is a clean paper, and capable of being governed by such laws as shall be found most agreeable to justice, and these may be so administered there as to afford a good precedent to England itself, where, when we shall once perceive that property may be preserved at so easy and cheap a rate, we shall never allow ourselves to be cheated and abused as we have been." It is not in the matter of conveyancing only that Ireland is a clean paper, where such laws may be tried as shall be most agreeable to justice and good precedents established for England herself.

Of Cromwell's colonial policy the records must be sought in colonial archives. The American historian, Mr. Bancroft, says : " Cromwell declared himself truly ready to serve the brethren and the churches in New England. The declaration was sincere. The people of New England were ever sure that Cromwell would listen to their requests and would take an interest in all the details of their condition. He left them independence and favoured their trade. When his arms had made the conquest of Jamaica he offered them the island, with the promise of all the wealth which the tropical

K

climate pours into the lap of industry, and
though they frequently thwarted his views they
never forfeited his regard." "English history,"
proceeds Mr. Bancroft, "must judge of Cromwell
by his influence on the institutions of England.
The American colonies remember the years of
his power as the period when British sovereignty
was, for them, free from rapacity, intolerance,
and oppression. He may be called the benefac-
tor of the English in America, for he left them
to enjoy unshackled the benevolence of Providence, the freedom of industry, of commerce,
of religion, and of government." Cromwell and
Chatham, these are the two English statesmen
the memory of whose sympathy America still
cherishes ; and were Cromwell and Chatham
"great un-Englishmen" and traitors to their
country ?

But it is to the foreign policy of Cromwell
that his country, even when she honoured
his name least, has always looked back with
a wistful eye. Unhappily it is a policy apt
not only to be admired but to be travestied
by wretched imitators when the age for it
is past. Such imitations are the mockery
and the bane of greatness. These are not

the days of commercial monopoly; Spain is
not now excluding the trade of all nations
from the western waters, and forcing them to
open the highroad of mercantile enterprise by
arms; nor is Europe now divided between
Catholicism and Protestantism, waging against
each other internecine war. The intense spirit
of narrow nationality produced by the disruption
of Christendom has now begun to give place
again, if not to a new Christendom, at least to
something like a community of nations. Cromwell's was a war policy; and so far as it was a
war policy, it was a bad policy, if Christianity
be true. But it was not a policy of mere aggrandisement. It was the championship of a
cause, a cause now out of date, but the best, the
purest, and the loftiest which the chief of Puritanism knew. Why did Cromwell league with
France against Spain when the power of Spain
was declining, when that of France was on the
point of rising to a height which threatened the
liberty of all nations? The answer is—first,
that the decline of Spain was scarcely yet
visible, even to the keenest eye; the vast dependencies, which we know now to have been
one cause of her decay, were still thought to be

the pillars of her towering greatness : secondly, that if Cromwell's dynasty had endured, the France of Louis XIV. would not have become the tyrant of Europe, for that which made her so was the prostration of England under the feet of the French king, and this was the work of the Restoration : but, thirdly, that Spain was the power of persecuting Catholicism, and that France, under Mazarin, though Catholic, was tolerant compared with Spain. To form a great Protestant league, and put England at its head again, was a policy which, unlike that of modern diplomatists, all the nation could understand, which carried the heart of the nation with it, and had the moral forces, as well as arms, upon its side. The Protector stepped into the place of Gustavus Adolphus, as the head of Protestant Christendom. The first embassy which he sent was to the daughter of Gustavus ; and Christina, before the madness which mingled with the heroic blood of Vasa had made her its prey, knew and acknowledged her father's heir. Her master of the ceremonies was not so kind ; but Whitelocke made his entry into the Swedish capital in a snowstorm, and it was a hard trial for a master of the ceremonies to stand bare-

headed in a snowstorm bowing to the ambassador of a regicide republic. A policy of mere
aggrandisement, without the championship of
a cause, is not a Cromwellian policy, nor are its
authors the heirs of Cromwell. Their meanness
stands contrasted with the majesty of the Protector. We have seen that, according to Mr.
Bancroft, Cromwell offered Jamaica to the
colonists of New England; and if he annexed
Dunkirk, it was in those ports that, within the
memory of living men, Parma had mustered his
army of invasion to be convoyed by the Armada.
Cromwell would have made England the head
at once of Protestantism and of Christendom.
As chief of Christendom, he chastised the pirates
of Tunis and Algiers, then the terror of christian
mariners on all seas. At home he was struggling for his government and his life with a
swarm of enemies; abroad, under his outstretched
arm, the Protestants of France and Savoy wor-
shipped God in peace. I am not an adherent of
non-intervention, if it means that England is to
have no sympathies, that she is never to inter-
pose for the defence of right or for the redress
of wrong. I believe that when she is again a
united nation, though she will not meddle or

bluster, she will make herself felt in the world
once more. Till she is united, no doubt she
must remain a nullity in Europe : no foreign
minister can act with effect, except as the organ
of the nation and with the nation at his back.
The case of the Protestants of Savoy stirred the
Protector's soul from its very depths : his feelings were expressed by the pen of Milton ; and
surely never did such a secretary serve such a
Prince in such a cause. Cromwell did not send
vapouring despatches ; he interposed effectually,
and right was done. He talked of making the
name of an Englishman as respected as that of
a Roman in a strain suited to those days, not
suited to ours. But he did not seek to win
respect for the English name by ignoble swag-
ger, or by trampling on the weak. He spared
the dignity even of the Duke of Savoy, though
if the Duke had refused justice, he would have
struck him to the dust.

The part of a conqueror, which Europe expected that Cromwell would assume in his own
person, his good sense at once renounced : and
on the evening of Worcester he sheathed his
sword for ever. Mr. Hallam, who was infected with the Whig worship of Napoleon,

speaks of his idol as the child of philosophy and of enlightenment, and contrasts him with Cromwell, who, he says, " had sucked the dregs of a besotted fanaticism." I find it difficult to conceive any fanaticism either so besotted or so cruel as that which leads a man to sacrifice the lives of millions and the happiness of hundreds of millions to his own " star."

" Cromwell," says Burnet, " studied to seek out able and honest men and to employ them, and so having heard that my father had a very good reputation in Scotland for piety and integrity, though he knew him to be a Royalist, he sent to him desiring him to accept a judge's place, and do justice in his own country, hoping only that he would not act against his government ; but he would not press him to subscribe or swear to it." This man had indeed a royal eye for merit and a royal heart to advance it in the state. Nor was he too nice in scrutinizing the opinions of able men, nor, so long as they served England well, did he too curiously inquire how they would serve him. Here again he stands contrasted with Bonaparte, whose first thought in advancing men was their subserviency to himself, who even

avoided promoting officers of the artillery, because that service had the character of being
republican.   There is no pledge of greatness so
rare, so decisive, or so noble as the choice of
associates who will not be tools.   Blake was
a Republican.   Lockhart, the chief instrument
of the Protector's foreign policy and the first
diplomatist of the day, was an old Royalist,
whose value Cromwell had discerned.   He was
employed again as ambassador at Paris under
Charles II., and still showed something of the
spirit of the Protectorate in altered times.   The
King of France once produced a private letter
from Charles, obtained by corrupt influence and
contrary to Lockhart's public instructions. "Sire,"
said Lockhart, " the King of England speaks to
your Majesty only through me."   Sir Matthew
Hale had been counsel to Strafford and the king :
and he well justified the Protector's choice by
boldly braving the wrath of the Protector himself, who, tried beyond endurance by the resistance to the establishment of his government,
had been betrayed into one of those brief out-
breaks of arbitrary violence which, though culp-
able in themselves, illustrated the more signally
his general desire to govern under the law.

Royal natures, even on a throne, love simplicity of life. The Protector kept such state
as became the head of a great nation, but it was
a modest state, unlike the tawdry pageantry of
the court of Bonaparte. A man of little refine-
ment and accustomed to the comradeship of the
camp, Cromwell in private was apt to relieve
his burdened mind with rude humour, boisterous
merriment, and even coarse practical jokes. But
when he received foreign ambassadors, he knew
how to show himself the head of a great nation
and the peer of kings. A leading part of his
entertainments was music, of which he was very
fond. The court was the first household in
England, and, as enemies confessed, a good pat-
tern to the others, let Mrs. Hutchinson in her
jealousy of the Cromwell women say what she
will. Whitehall was the scene of work. But
sometimes the Protector shuffled off that terrible
coil of business and anxiety, and his lifeguards
waited to escort him (their escort was no need-
less pageantry) in his ride to Hampton Court.
There he refreshed his soul with quiet and
country air. Thither an organ had been brought
from the chapel of Magdalen College at Oxford,
to chase away for an hour the throng of cares.

But the Protector's chief comfort and delight was in his family, to which through all the chances and changes of his life, in trial alike and in victory, his heart had turned. They were all gathered round him in the hour of his greatness and of his peril, and remained bound by strong affection to him and to each other. One was missing, the eldest son, Oliver, who had fallen in battle for the cause, and whose image, as we know from Cromwell's last utterances, never left his father's heart. Among the rest the Protector's mother, ninety years old, was brought to a scene strange to her and in which she had little comfort, for every report of a gun she heard seemed to her her son's death, and she could not bear to pass a day without seeing him with her own eyes. We may trust the brief account of her end which is found among the dry state papers of the unimaginative Thurloe :—" My Lord Protector's mother, ninety-four years old, died last night. A little before her death she gave my lord her blessing in these words : ' The Lord cause His face to shine upon you and comfort you in all your adversities, and enable you to do great things for the glory of your most High God, and to be a relief unto His people. My dear son, I leave my heart with thee. A good night.' "

I have estimated Cromwell highly. I see no reason why his nation in his age should not in the terrible but fruitful throes of a revolution have brought forth one of the greatest of the sons of men. "A larger soul never dwelt in a house of clay," said one who had been much about his person, after his death, when flattery was mute. His greatness is not to be compared to that of conquerors. Ten years more of Alexander and we should have had ten more satrapies. Ten years more of Napoleon and we should have had ten more conquests at once profligate and insensate, civilization put back ten degrees more, the barbarous war spirit made ten degrees more powerful in the world. Ten years more of Cromwell and the history of England and of Europe might have been changed. In England we should have had no revival of the absolutist and Romanising monarchy of the Stuarts ; no resurrection of the Cavalier party under the name of Tories ; no waste of the energies of the nation and disturbance of its progress by the renewal of that barren struggle ; no restoration of the hierarchy ; and if an hereditary House of Lords, one at all events that could not have fancied itself Norman, and must almost inevitably have assumed more of the character of a national Senate. In Europe, there would have been no domination of Louis XIV. ; no extermination of French Protestantism ; probably no such crisis as that of the French Revolution.

And now the Protector's foot was on the threshold of success. His glory, the excellence of his administration, his personal dignity and virtues were founding his government in the allegiance of the people. The friends of order were beginning to perceive that their best chance of order lay in giving stability to his throne. Some of the great families, acting on this view, had connected themselves by marriage with his house. His finances were embarrassed ; but he was about again to meet a Parliament which would probably have voted him supplies and concurred with him in settling the constitution. His foot was on the threshold of success ; but on the threshold of success stood Death. It was death in a strange form for him : for after all his battles and storms and all the plots of assassins against his life, this terrible chief died of grief at the loss of his favourite daughter and of watching at her side.

Up that steep and slippery path of worldly greatness, so dangerous to the simplicity of faith and virtue, the religious farmer of Huntingdon-shire had wandered far away from the Puritanism of his youth. He felt it, and when his end was near he asked his chaplain whether those who had once been in a state of grace could fall from it. He was assured that they could not. Then he said, " I am saved, for I am sure that I was once in a state of grace." The Calvinistic formula has become obsolete for most of us : but we may still trust that he who has once sincerely devoted himself to God's service is not often allowed to become an enemy of God.

At the time of his installation, the Protector had executed the power given him by Parlia-ment of naming a successor. He had sealed up the paper and addressed it to Thurloe, but had kept both the paper and its secret to himself. In his last illness, at Hampton Court, he sent to London for the paper, telling the messenger that it was on his study-table at Whitehall ; but the paper could not be found. Whose name did it contain ? I doubt not, that of Richard

Cromwell. Perhaps the Protector's memory had failed him, and he had really destroyed the paper, still expecting that Richard would succeed not as Protector under the power of nomination, but by act of Parliament as hereditary king. Nor do I see any reason to question Thurloe's statement that the Protector named Richard his successor by word of mouth just before he died. What else was to be done? Richard was weak, as his father must too well have known; but he was popular and blameless, and had the shadow of hereditary right. Henry Cromwell was a man of mark as well as of worth, but not of mark enough to bear the burden unsupported by any other claim. Among the generals there was not one to be thought of since Ireton was gone. We know the rest. How military ambition broke loose: how anarchy ensued. Anarchy, not Cromwell's government, brought on the Restoration. At last the nobler spirit of the nation rose again. But the Revolution of 1688 was an aristocratic revolution ; and there were other interests for which men had given their lives at Marston and Naseby, and with which, when Cromwell died before his time, all was over for many a day.

All was over here, and once more there was an illustration of the frailty of systems and institutions which depend on a single life. But the counsels of Providence never depend upon a single life. Just as the great struggle was commencing in England, a little bark put forth on the Atlantic, unnoticed amidst the great events and the great actors of the time. Its passengers were Puritan peasants, hunted out of their homes by the Anglican hierarchy and its persecuting agents. It bore English Democracy, safe beyond the reach of the English reaction, to the shores of the New World. There, too, it has encountered its old foes, the enemies of liberty, both of body and soul. But there it has triumphed : it has triumphed for itself, and it has triumphed for us all.

PITT.

III.

P I T T. — I.

THE European movement which ended in the French Revolution, like that which ended in the Reformation, like all great movements of humanity, was complex in its nature. It was at once religious and political, and it extended to all the other parts of human life. In religion it was almost entirely critical and destructive. To our generation was left the heavy task of renovating faith. The religion of Rousseau, indeed, proved itself the strongest among the elements which struggled for mastery in the Revolution. We can understand how at the time it breathed in its freshness like the breath of morning into the feverish atmosphere of French life. But it was merely a bastard Christianity, emotional, sentimental, based on no conviction. The great service done to religion during the eighteenth century was the advancement of toleration, to which Frederic the great, tyrant as he was in politics, was a real friend; though it was the toleration of indifference, not the toleration of those, who with deep convictions, and because they have deep convictions, reverence conscience as the source, and liberty of conscience as the sole guarantee, of truth. In the political sphere also the movement was merely destructive; it pulled down feudalism without building up anything in its place, and it has left European society generally in a chaotic state, from which the nations have sought refuge in democratic despotism, pending the evolution of a sound and permanent order of things. Two political ideals, however, this century produced; the half-classical, half-Christian Republicanism of Rousseau, and the enlightened and beneficent despotism, having its imaginary type in China, which was the Utopia of Voltaire. In jurisprudence and political economy, on the other hand, there were positive and great results: in jurisprudence, the reforms of law, especially the law of succession to property and the penal code, of which the Code Napoleon is the most scientific embodiment, though the philosophy of the previous century was the source; in economy, free trade, and all the benefits which the world has received from the principles enunciated by Hume, Turgot, and, greatest of all, Adam Smith.

The first part of Pitt's life—that part which forms the subject of this evening's lecture—is a product of the economical, and in some measure also of the political, part of this European movement, limited by the conditions imposed on the leader of an aristocratic assembly and a minister of the English crown ; the second part, which will form the subject of the following lecture, is a product of the reaction against the religious and political part of the same movement when it had arrived at its revolutionary crisis and overturned the French Church and Throne. During the first part of his life, Pitt is to be classed with the philosophic and reforming kings and ministers before the Revolution, whose names ought not to be forgotten, though the Jacobins chose to call the year of their frenzy the year One ; with Joseph II. ; with Pombal, Aranda, and Choiseul, the overthrowers of Jesuitism ; with Tanucci, with Leopold of Tuscany, with Turgot, with Frederic of Prussia, and with Catherine of Russia, so far as Catherine and Frederic were organs of philosophy and reform.

During the second part, he tends, though he does not actually sink, to the level of the Metternichs, the Polignacs, the Percevals, and the Eldons. The Pitt of my present lecture and the Pitt of my next stand in strong contrast to each other, though the connection is quite intelligible and signally illustrates the power of circumstances over any but the strongest men. The same change is seen in the lives of Joseph and Catherine and other reformers in high places, who, when the Revolution came, found out that their trade was that of king. It is seen in the English aristocracy, the more intellectual of whom had, like the French aristocracy, been affecting scepticism and Republicanism, as we may learn from Horace Walpole, who is always throwing out light Voltairian sentiments and cutting off the head of Charles I. This evening we speak of the happier Pitt, of him whose monuments remain in free trade, an improved fiscal system, religious toleration, the first steps towards colonial emancipation, the abolition of the slave trade, the condemnation of slavery. Another evening we shall speak of the Pitt whose monuments remain in six hundred millions of debt, and other evils political and social, of which the bitter inheritance has descended to us and will descend to generations yet to come.

William Pitt was born beneath a roof illustrious, but not likely to give birth to an apostle of economical reform. What the inglorious frugality of Walpole had saved, Chatham had squandered in victory; and he had added a heavy burden of debt besides. But the father bequeathed to his child the example of purity, of patriotism, of a high aspiring spirit, which soared, if not to the summit of political heroism, at least far above the place-hunters and intriguers of the time. He bequeathed to him also of his eloquence, not the incommunicable fire, but so much as assiduous culture under a great master could impart, and sent him into public life a youthful prodigy in the accomplishment by which we choose our statesmen. From the conversation of Chatham and of Chatham's friends, Pitt, who was brought up at home, must also have learned much; and thus his parliamentary maturity at twenty-one, though a wonder, is not a miracle.

I have noticed that Pitt was brought up at home. He was nevertheless no milksop. We complacently accept it as a full set-off against all the evils of public schools, that they make boys manly. It is easy to see how by cutting boys off from intercourse with men and women, and confining them to the society of boys, you may make them hard; but not so easy to see how you can make them manly. Pitt brought up in the house of Chatham is, of course, too exceptional a case to reason from : but no want of manliness, either of mind or character, was seen in this boy when he became Prime Minister at twenty-four.

He, however, went to Cambridge at fourteen, and stayed there seven years, during which he was regular and read hard, owing, it may be, partly to the weakness of his health, which by debarring from physical sports and enjoyments, has perhaps turned not a few men into the path which leads to intellectual greatness. We are beginning to know the power of education, and the significance of the question, what sort of culture it was that was undergone by a future chief of the state. The classics, a school at once of taste and of the political character formed by a rather narrow and heathen love of liberty, were the staple of Pitt's training, as they had been those of the English statesmen before him.

To these he added the discipline of mathematics, some jurisprudence, some experimental philosophy, and a good deal of general literature, including history. Historical philosophy was not then in existence : it might have taught him, the destined ruler of his country at the epoch of the French Revolution, to view with intelligence and meet with calmness the tremendous phenomena of his time. But above all he read the work, then new and unknown to his elder rivals, of Adam Smith, to which, in his great budget-speech of 1792, he referred as furnishing the best solution to every question connected with political economy and with trade. Pitt was Adam Smith's first powerful disciple. And from this source he drew not only the principles of his commercial reforms and his budgets, but a talisman of command. The commercial and manufacturing interests were rapidly rising in importance, and with these interests Pitt alone of the party leaders had qualified himself to deal. The aristocratic statesmen, with their purely classical training, seldom stooped to anything so low as economy or finance. Fox avowed his ignorance of political economy ; he used to say he did not know why the funds went up or down, but he liked to see them go down because it vexed Pitt. Sir Francis Dashwood was thought good enough for the Chancellorship of the Exchequer, though a sum of five figures was said to be an inscrutable mystery to his mind. The student of the "Wealth of Nations" might have learnt, and perhaps he did learn, from it, other things besides those which he mentioned in his budget-speech. Free principles hang together, and Adam Smith is, in an unobtrusive way, the apostle of Democracy as well as of Free Trade.

Pitt's tutor was Pretyman, better known in the annals of ecclesiastical rapacity by his later name of Tomline. This man seems to have done the classical and mathematical part of his duty well: Pitt at least was grateful to him, and gorged him—to satiate him was impossible—with preferment, till George III. cried "Hold, enough." Tomline thus enriched, provided with the means of enriching his whole tribe, and having inherited a private fortune besides, subscribed, among others, £1,000 towards the payment of Pitt's debts, which sum he afterwards tried to get repaid to him by the nation.

Bad physicians advised the stripling to drink port, the panacea and almost the physical gospel of the age ; and he followed their advice with a vengeance. Hence disease and mortal langour in his prime ; hence the constitution early decayed which succumbed to the blow of Austerlitz. Lord Stanhope—to whose most valuable biography, which forms the foundation of this lecture, let me here acknowledge my great obligations—Lord Stanhope says that Pitt was only once seen drunk. There are traditions of a different kind. In all other respects Pitt's character, like that of his great father, was pure ; and though the wits might scoff at the idea that genius and morality could exist together, his purity gave him a great advantage in self-control, in conscientious industry, in dignity of bearing, in the confidence of the community— especially of the middle classes—over his chief rival, who, though he had a warm heart and noble sympathies, was a rake, a gambler, corrupt himself, and a corrupter of the youths about him. Of religion there was little to be had in those days ; and of that little not much resided in Mr. Pretyman. Pitt was regular in his attendance at the college chapel. He also read theology with his tutor, and some would have us believe that he became a theologian at once most learned and most orthodox, armed at all points to maintain the Thirty-nine Articles against all heresies, whether on the side of Popery or Dissent; while, on the other hand, there is a tradition that, by his own avowal, Butler's "Analogy" raised in his mind more doubts than it solved, wherein he would by no means have been unique. But it is plain that he had not that strong and present sense of things unseen by which the noblest characters have been sustained. So far as integrity and real desire of the public good would carry him, he could go : but when the great trial came, the trial which called for complete self-sacrifice, the sustaining force was wanting, conscience yielded to ambition, and the son of the morning fell.

As Chatham's son, Pitt entered public life as a Whig. But Whig, by this time, meant little more than Guelf or Ghibelin. The Whigs were a party, and an illustrious party, while they were making the Revolution of 1688, and afterwards while they were defending the Revolution settlement against Louis XIV. abroad and the Jacobites at home. But that struggle

over, they became an oligarchy of great houses
squabbling among themselves for the high
offices of state. The long scene of degradation
which ensued had, for a time, been broken by
the rise of Chatham, a middle-class minister
putting the oligarchy under his feet, though
to do it he was obliged himself to connive at
corruption, and allow a Duke to do for his
government the work which the great Com-
moner abhorred. In this party government
of ours, which we take for an eternal ordinance
of nature, though it is but an accident of yesterday, everything depends on the existence of
a real division of opinion on some important
question. When the great questions are for
the time out of the way, party government
degenerates into a chronic faction-fight between
a connection which wants to get place and a
connection which wants to keep it. At this
time the great questions were out of the way,
there was no real division of parties, and a
reign of cabal and corruption naturally ensued.
All the factions alike used power for class
purposes; the nation had little interest in their
scuffles, and no hope but that by some accident
a man of heart and brain might get into his

hands a measure of independent power, and use it partly for the public good.

Pitt took his seat when only just of age for the nomination borough of Appleby, and at once came forward in debate. His command of rounded sentences was already fearful; assuredly no youth ever wrote such stately despatches to his mother. He gave the House without delay a taste of his oratoric training, and early showed his greatest gift as an orator, the power of lofty sarcasm, which, in a House not much in earnest, is so telling, both in its direct effect, and because, unlike open invective, it suggests a reserve of power. Those stately speeches of his, with their long rolling periods, were, no doubt, very imposing when they were delivered with an imperial bearing and haughty gestures from the summit of Parliamentary command. But the best of them, and those best reported, can scarcely be placed in the small number of orations which deserve to live beyond the hour. They contain few memorable words. That fusion of reason in the fire of passion, the attribute of the highest eloquence, is not there. They are the works of talent, but not of genius.

The war with the American Colonies had

almost run its guilty and disastrous course, and
was drawing near its shameful end. The North
ministry tottered to its fall. It was upheld
only by the personal support of the King, who,
like kings in general, was still for war. Pitt
went into strong opposition. He denounced the
war with a vehemence which, we should have
thought, would have seemed inexpiable to the
King. He supported Burke's motion for re-
trenchment. He took up Parliamentary Reform
warmly, and made the question his own. This
he did with his guns levelled directly against
the corrupt influence of the court—" an influence," he said, " which has been pointed at in
every period as the fertile source of all our
miseries—an influence which has been substi-
tuted in the· room of wisdom, of activity, of
exertion, and of success—an influence which
has grown with our growth, and strengthened
with our strength, but which unhappily has not
diminished with our diminution, nor decayed
with our decay." The court was so discredited
and detested that on his motion for a select committee Pitt was only beaten by 20. It has been
remarked that the Reformers never had so good
a division again till 1831. Pitt also voted for

the motion of the Radical Alderman Sawbridge
to shorten the duration of parliaments. If this
bright archangel of Toryism had sat long in
opposition he might have become a minister of
the Darker Power.

North fell ; and over the prostrate favourite
of the court Fox and Rockingham entered the
royal closet by storm.   On Rockingham's death
Fox pressed the Duke of Portland on the King
as first minister, but the King carried Lord
Shelburne, one of Chatham's old connection ; and
Pitt, whose aspiring boyhood had refused office
without a seat in the cabinet under Rockingham, came into Shelburne's cabinet at twenty-
three as Chancellor of the Exchequer. The foot
of Adam Smith was on the steps of power.

The Shelburne ministry had to make peace
with the Americans, and with their allies,
France and Spain : but on the preliminaries of
peace the Government was overthrown by the
profligate coalition of Fox and North. Profligate that coalition was, not so much because
it violated political principle, for none of these
factions had much political principle to violate,
as because it violated personal honour. Fox
had spoken of North in terms which made an

alliance between them, manifestly concluded for the sake of getting back into place, equally infamous to them both. The king struggled; he turned to Pitt; and the dazzling offer of the premiership was refused by a farsighted youth of twenty-three. Then the king was forced to go under the yoke: but this time the nation was with him, and his defeat was a moral victory.

A constitutional monarchy, according to the classic aphorism of M. Thiers, is one in which the king reigns and does not govern; in the less pointed words of Lord North, one in which the king has only the appearance of power. This highly artificial arrangement—for highly artificial it is, when we consider that the king is treated, even in our addresses to Heaven, as though he were the real ruler, and we his obedient subjects—is commonly taken to be coeval with the monarchy of England. It came into existence a century and a half ago, and has not continued without interruption since that time. The feudal kings, like the Saxon kings before them, not only reigned but governed, and were deposed, and sometimes put to death, if they governed ill. The Tudors were despots.

M

The Stuarts tried to be. William III., though a foreigner, and dependent on the Whigs for his crown, was at the head of his own government, had no foreign minister but himself, at a time when foreign policy was the most important department, and vetoed the Triennial Act. Anne changed the government and the policy of the country at the whim of her waiting-woman. The first constitutional king was George I., a foreigner like William, very stupid, which William was not, unable to speak English, with a Pretender across the water, and absolutely in the hands of his Whig patrons. George II. was pretty much in the same case, and accordingly he was only one degree less constitutional than his father. But George III., as he told Parliament in graceful compliment to the shades of his ancestors, was born a Briton. "What lustre," responded the Peers, "does it add to the name of Briton when you, Sir, esteem it among your glories." Jacobinism was defunct; and the last nonjuring bishop died about this time, an apothecary at Shrewsbury, owning that Providence had declared itself for the Hanover line. Therefore, George III. was not constitutional: he wished not only to reign but to govern.

He is surely not much to be blamed for that
wish. Hearing a prayer put up every Sunday,
that he might be enabled to rule well, he might
not unnaturally conceive that it was a part of
his duty to rule. Despotic ideas had been care-
fully infused by his mother and Lord Bute into
a mind which the absence of any other culture
left entirely open for their reception; for never
had a born Briton so un-British an education.
The Parliament of that day was not a free Parliament, but an oligarchical and rotten-borough
Parliament; and we might have sympathised
with the King if he had really intended to over-
ride the factions, put the oligarchy under the
feet of a national trustee, promote merit in the
public service without regard to connection, and
govern in the interest of the whole nation.
Unfortunately, George the Third's idea of merit
was Lord Bute and Mr Jenkinson, and his idea
of governing in the interest of the whole nation
was the American war. It was unlucky, too,
if the new system was to restore purity, that it
was itself supported by corruption; and that in
this corruption, and in the coarsest form of it—
that connected with elections—the King himself took an active part. If any one, in his

hatred of oligarchy, dreams of a patriot king, let him awake from that dream. Sooner than a patriot king, he will find an oligarchy ready to divest itself of power.

George III. tried unconstitutional monarchy, first by Lord Bute, a walking-gentleman, and failed; then by Lord North, a good man of business and a good parliamentary tactician, but pliant enough to submit to government by departments; that is, a government in which the king was first minister, and the departments against their consciences carried on the King's American war. But the end of that war brought the system to the ground amidst a storm of odium; and only the superior odium of the Coalition could have given the King a third chance. A third chance he now had, and having twice before got hold of a tool who was not strong enough to be a minister, he now got hold of a minister who was rather too strong to be a tool.

The Coalition deserved to fall, but not on the measure on which it fell. It had become necessary for humanity, and for the honour of the country, to arrest the servants of the East India Company in their career of crime. The govern-

ment brought in a bill taking India out of the
hands of the Company and putting it into the
hands of a board of seven commissioners to be
named for the first time by parliament and
afterwards by the crown. There can be no
doubt that the measure was framed in good
faith. Burke, whose zeal for Indian reform
none will question, was its framer. Fox himself, with all his faults, was a true friend of
humanity : let us honour his name for it, at
a time when contempt for humanity and sympathy with cruelty is cultivated by feebleness
as a proof of vigour, and lauded by public in-
structors as a healthy English tone. As, however, the majority in parliament were to have
the nominations for the first time, a cry was got
up that the party intended, by the appropriation
of overwhelming patronage, to perpetuate itself
in power. Set up by Pitt and the opposition,
this cry was swelled of course by the whole
East Indian interest, which by buying rotten
boroughs had made itself a great parliamentary
power, and was beginning, in the secret counsels
of Providence, to avenge, by its pestilential influence on English politics, the wrongs of the
Hindoo. The great standing army, estranged

from the ideas of English citizenship and from reverence for English liberties, which is now being trained up in India, may perhaps one day carry further the work of retribution, and teach people that they cannot practise rapine in another country, even under pretence of propagating Christianity, and with the tacit sanction of their bishops, without entailing some consequences on their own.   The king was in a paroxysm of rage and fear at the prospect of having so much power taken out of his hands. The bill, however, passed the Commons by a large majority, and was on the point of passing the Lords, when Lord Temple, who had before been carrying on a most unconstitutional correspondence with the King against the Ministers, crept to the royal ear, and received from His Majesty a paper to be handed about among the Lords in the following terms : " His Majesty allowed Earl Temple to say that whoever voted for the India Bill was not only not his friend but would be considered by him as an enemy ; and if these words were not strong enough, Earl Temple might use whatever words he deemed stronger and more to the purpose." The only words which could have been stronger and more to the purpose would have been some having reference to more substantial motives than affection for the royal person. By a free use of this august document, the India Bill was thrown out ; and the Coalition ministers fell, most of them in transports of rage, Lord North, with his usual good-humour, declining to get out of bed at twelve o'clock at night to give up the seals, and forcing the royal envoy, who came at that unseasonable hour, to have an interview with Lady North, as well as with himself. For a moment, Temple, the author of the plot, was secretary of state ; but he immediately vanished under a cloud of mystery which has never been cleared away. Lord Stanhope is inclined to think that Lord Temple having saved the monarchy by a back-stairs intrigue, wished to assure its salvation by getting himself made a Duke ; and that the King, faithful to first principles, even in this supreme hour of political extremity, would make none but Royal Dukes. A more obvious solution is that Temple, like most intriguers, was a coward, and that his heart failed him as he touched his prize. What is certain is, that Lord Temple went to Stowe. Meanwhile the King had turned again to Pitt ;

and Pitt was prime minister, and not only prime minister, but, as the rest of the cabinet were mere respectabilities, sole minister at twenty-four.

Unluckily there was now a taint on his appointment, which there would not have been if he had dared to accept the prime minister-ship before. Lord Stanhope defends the King and his partners in this transaction. He says the rules of the constitution were not then settled. The principle that the King was not to take notice of anything depending in Parlia-ment had been asserted, as I apprehend, against the Stuarts. But be this as it may, if the rules of the constitution were not settled, the rules of honour were ; and the rules of honour, while they permitted the King to dismiss his minis-ters openly and appeal against them to the country, did not permit him to stab them in the dark. But, says Lord Stanhope, Pitt at all events stands clear. His conduct was excusable perhaps ; but if the transaction was criminal, he was not guiltless. He was an accomplice after the fact. He screened Lord Temple in parliament. He accepted the fruits of the intrigue. Afterwards, he was himself called upon to confront the prejudices of the King. George III. was cunning, and though he might quail before the haughty son of Chatham, he must have felt in his heart that Pitt had once been his accomplice.

Then came the famous struggle of the young minister at the head of a minority, and without a colleague to support him in the House of Commons, against the superior forces and the veteran chiefs of the Coalition. The merit of Pitt in this struggle has been overrated. The Opposition made him a present of the victory. They should have proceeded not passionately but vigorously against Temple, and treated Pitt with cool forbearance, so as to avoid making him an object of national sympathy. They proceeded passionately but by no means vigorously against Temple, and they assailed Pitt with a ferocity which arrayed the sympathies of all men on his side. The fact is, however, that Pitt played a winning game from the beginning. The numbers of the majority in the House were no measure of their hold on the country. The nation was weary of cabals which bandied power from one set of place-hunters to another. Its heart yearned towards the young, and as it

hóped pure and patriotic, son of Chatham. The
Tories wished the King to choose his own
ministers. The few Radicals that there were
hated the great Whig houses. The Coalition
was hated by all.

In the middle of the struggle the Clerkship
of the Pells (a sinecure office with an income of
£3,000 a year) fell vacant. The minister might
have taken it himself, and Pitt was poor.
He fancied that if he lost his place he should
have to go back to the bar. But he used the
windfall to redeem a pension which had been
improperly bestowed by the other party, thus
placing his own purity in contrast with their
corruption. As a minister he waged no war on
great sinecures, and he held the Wardenship of
the Cinque Ports himself. But this act proved
at least that he was playing a high game, and
that he would not let his cupidity stand in the
way of his ambition. He shewed sagacity, too,
in putting off the dissolution, and thus giving
the opposition rope to hang themselves, and the
tide of opinion time to rise in his favour. Even
in the House, the Opposition was at the last
gasp; and when urged by its leaders to throw
out the Mutiny Bill, it no longer answered the

spur. A last effort was made by a devoted
adherent in the falling hour of the great Whig
houses. The day before the dissolution some-
body stole the Great Seal. But the fortitude
and resource of the young minister were equal
to the occasion, and a new Great Seal was at
once made.

When Pitt at last went to the country, there
was a rout of the Opposition never paralleled
except when the Whigs, in their turn, threw the
Tories to the reformed constituencies in 1832.
The great majority with which Pitt returned
to the House was a medley, in which high
Tories were mixed up with Alderman Sawbridge
and John Wilkes. But he rapidly gave it consistency by making his name the symbol of
prosperity and sound finance, and by attaching
commerce, whose interests he alone understood,
firmly to his banner. Soon he was all-powerful,
and the beginning of his reign is an epoch in
our history. There had been no revolution. All
the cabinet were peers except Pitt himself; and
he was an earl's son. He had come into power
by the personal favour of the King. He could
do nothing against the King or his order. But
with these restrictions, he wished to rule for the

public good.   His intellect was probably not so high as that of Turgot, but it was more practical : and his task was not, like that of Turgot, almost hopeless.   Bright years, years bright for himself—and, on the whole, bright for his country—lay before him.   Such a part can scarcely ever be played again.   In ordinary times, connection and experience must rule.   But it is possible that, under certain circumstances, the House of Commons may once more weary and disgust the nation ;   and that a statesman of high bearing and known public spirit may once more appeal with success from cabal and faction to the heart of the people.

The highly aristocratic composition of Pitt's Cabinet is a proof that there had been no revolution : it has also been justly cited as one of the many confutations of the theory that the Tories are less oligarchical than the Whigs. Under the influence of this theory, Lord Stanhope, a moderate Tory, sometimes lapses into language fundamentally democratic.   " In 1784 the independent freeholders of Yorkshire boldly confronted the great houses"—this is an appeal to a dangerous spirit, unless care is taken to insert "Tory" before " freeholders," and " Whig "

before "great houses." The fact seems to be
that the Tories being, through some cause un-
explained by political science, rather more stupid
than the Whigs, have been rather more often
obliged to take adventurers into pay ; but they
do this for oligarchical purposes, and an oligarch
is not the less an oligarch because he keeps a
bravo.

The young conqueror sullied his triumph by
most ungenerous conduct to his rival on the
subject of the Westminster Scrutiny. He had
the mortification, as deserved as it was bitter,
of finding himself at last placed in a minority
by the more generous feeling of his own followers. In one of these debates, which, in spite
of the aristocratic character of the speakers,
were as rancorous and personal as anything in
an American Congress, Fox made a really great
speech, in which he read his young rival a well-
merited lecture on the expediency of moderation in the use of victory. Nothing can exceed
the pertness and bad taste of Pitt's reply—
" I am not surprised if he should pretend to
be the butt of ministerial persecution ; and if,
by striving to excite the public compassion,
he should seek to reinstate himself in that

popularity which he once enjoyed, but which he
so unhappily has forfeited. For it is the best
and most ordinary resource of these political
apostates to court and offer themselves to persecution, for the sake of the popular predilection
and pity which usually fall upon persecuted
men; it becomes worth their while to suffer
for a time political martyrdom, for the sake of
the canonisation that awaits the suffering
martyr; and I make no doubt the right honourable gentleman has so much penetration, and at
the same time so much passive virtue about
him, that not only would he be glad to seem a
poor, injured, persecuted man, but he would
gladly seek an opportunity of even really suffering a little persecution, if it be possible to
find such an opportunity." It must have been
difficult for an opponent, or for any one indeed
but a partisan, to help very cordially abhorring
the gifted youth, from whose lips flowed un-
bidden such perfect periods as these; especially
when at his back was a mob of Tory squires,
under the famous Rolle, hooting down the
speakers on the other side—a habit perhaps not
yet quite extinct. If there was any one in that
assembly to whom the term apostate might

with justice have been applied, it was the
vehement advocate of Parliamentary Reform as
the great antidote to secret influence who now
stood, through a most flagrant exercise of secret
influence, First Minister of the Crown.

Pitt's great glories are economical and financial. In that sphere, as he touched neither prerogative nor privilege, royalty and aristocracy
allowed him to have free play. They even
formed his support in contending against the
commercial tyranny of protection.

He found the finances after the American war
and the North Administration in a desperate
state. There were 14 millions of unfunded
debt; exchequer bills were at 20 discount;
consols were at 56. The customs were so laid
on that the smuggling trade in tea was double
the lawful trade in amount. The pupil of Adam
Smith set all this right, brought income by bold
taxation to a level with expenditure, and applying the principle which he was the first to grasp—
that reduction of duties will increase revenue by
increasing consumption—transferred the gains
of the smuggler to the national exchequer. He
was at the same time enabled to do away with
a number of places in the Customs and Excise,

and thereby not only to reduce the national expense, but to stanch some of the sources of corruption. He thus, in spite of some occasional waste in armaments, the debts of the Prince of Wales, and the voracity of the civil list, turned deficit into surplus, and saved England perhaps from a crash like that to which deficit was hurrying France. He was also the author of the reform which put up loans to the highest bidder, instead of making them government patronage, with a toll to corruption.

Adam Smith had denounced funding. His pupil, when obliged to borrow, borrowed in the five rather than in the three per cents, to keep down the capital debt and improve the chance of paying off. He had not read Lord Macaulay, who from the growth of suburban villas "embosomed in gay little paradises of lilacs and roses," proves that a funded debt of eight hundred millions is no burden to the nation. He had not learnt that in the case of a national debt, debtor and creditor are the same, so that, as it seems, we might as well simplify the transaction by the use of the sponge. Still less, probably, had he, like Lord Macaulay, discerned the recondite truth, that the practice of fighting with soldiers hired at the expense of posterity, which removes the last restraint on war, is favourable to the ascendancy of intellect over force. He might have asked Lord Macaulay, if a national debt was a blessing, why it should not be doubled ?

In his anxiety to reduce the debt Pitt was caught by the project of a sinking fund. When national debts grew heavy, various projects were devised in different countries for conjuring them away without the unpleasant process of paying. The Mississippi scheme and the South Sea scheme were among the number. Tampering with the currency was a coarse expedient. The simplest was that of the French Finance Minister, Abbé Terrai, who repudiated fifty per cent, and proved that the glory of repudiation is not monopolised by republics. The sinking fund was a project for conjuring away the debt by the magic of compound interest. People think that money at compound interest grows of itself like a plant. But compound interest, in the case of individuals, is merely compound savings reinvested, and compound diversions of capital from other investments. In the case of a national sinking fund it is compound payments

N

made by the nation to itself. Of course, as soon as the question arises between further borrowing, perhaps at a high rate of interest, for some pressing emergency, and dipping into the sinking fund, the sinking fund goes to the wall. There are only three courses for nations which have run into debt—to bear the debt for ever, to become bankrupt, or to remain at peace, retrench and pay.

It does seem, however, that a nation ought to take advantage of its immortality, and to borrow on terminable rather than on perpetual annuities. To the mortal creditor there is no difference between an annuity for the longest span of mortal interest and an annuity for ever. To the immortal nation there is, between a burden for a century and a burden for ever, all the difference in the world.

Destiny mocks the hopes of man. This is the minister of whom it was too truly said— " Mr. Pitt's memory needs no statues. Six hundred millions of irredeemable debt are the eternal record of his fame." He ought, from his early studies and experiences, to have felt more strongly the injustice of laying burdens on other generations without their own consent. In barbarous ages, people when they went to war fought themselves. Civilisation taught them to hire, impress, or kidnap other people to fight for them. Still there was a check on war while those who made it had to pay. Taxation of the present was confined within narrow limits; it provoked unpleasant outcries, sometimes it provoked resistance. So the expedient was hit upon of taxing the mute and unresisting future. The system was perfected by degrees. At first the Government only anticipated payments which they might, with some colour of reason, call their own. Then they mortgaged particular sources of revenue. Funding with us dates from William III.; hence to the author of the great Whig epic, of which William is the Achilles, the system seems all lilacs and roses.

Pitt's financial speeches were as notable as his budgets. Inferior, no doubt, in knowledge to those of Peel, they are superior in form, which is something when people are to be instructed on a subject to most men at once repulsive and obscure.

In the mind of Pitt, as in that of Adam Smith, as in that of Cobden, as in the counsels of Providence, free trade was connected with a policy of peace and goodwill among nations. Pitt, too, was " an international man.". Since the religious wars of the sixteenth century, hatred had been the law of Christendom. International malignity had been organised under the name of the Balance of Power. Each nation had thought itself prosperous just so far as it could prevent the prosperity of others. Hence protection, the colonial system, and commercial as well as diplomatic wars. Chatham's glory had been bound up with these notions, especially with the notion of eternal enmity between England and France. But Chatham's son, enlightened by a better teacher, commenced the work of healing, through free commercial intercourse, the divisions of Christendom. The precursor of Cobden, he carried, against strong opposition, a commercial treaty with France. Fox was a man of larger sympathies than Pitt, and if he had been in power would probably have been on the whole a better foreign minister ; but party, sacred party, hurried him and his liberal friends into denouncing the treaty on the most illiberal grounds of international jealousy. In defending it, Pitt combated, in language which Cobden might have used, the

doctrine that France must be the unalterable
enemy of Britain. He treated as monstrous,
and as founded neither in nature nor in history,
the position that one nation could be the
unalterable enemy of another. He called it a
libel on society, as supposing the existence of
diabolical malice in the original frame of man.
He was obliged to pay some homage to the war
spirit, as in truth does Adam Smith; and he
urges that whatever enriches us will, when the
time comes, give us the sinews of war. But he
returns to less equivocal ground in showing that
the chances of war will be diminished when
nations are bound together by free trade. The
chances of war will be diminished. Let us not,
in the face of so many victories of principle,
honour, passion over mere interest, imagine that
any bond of mere interest can do more. If to
slake a fierce hatred or to uphold a great cause
men will sacrifice their lives, much more will
they for a time sacrifice the luxuries for which
they are dependent on foreign trade. The only
sure guarantee of peace is morality. The next
greatest is not commerce but freedom, which
puts down standing armies. A commercial
treaty is a poor set-off against the mischief done

by a military despotism, the great embodiment and consecration of the war spirit in the world : and if we were to truck our abhorrence of military despotism for such a treaty, we should find—to put the question on the lowest ground —that we had bought our mess of pottage far too dear.

Adam Smith had advocated the union of Ireland with England. He had pointed out that free trade with England would far more than make up to Ireland for the increase of taxation—that by the union of his own country with England, the Scotch people had been delivered from the Scotch aristocracy—that by the same process Ireland " might be delivered from a much more oppressive aristocracy, an aristocracy the most odious of all, an aristocracy of political and religious prejudice, which, more than any other distinctions, animated the insolence of the oppressor and the hatred of the oppressed, and made the natives of the same country greater enemies than those of different countries ever were." At this time the relations between Ireland and England were such as could not be endured. The Protestant Republicans of the North of Ireland—they, mind, not the Catholics—taking advantage of the weakness of England after her reverses in the American war, and catching the infection of the American Revolution, had risen in arms, under pretence of forming a volunteer army for the defence of the kingdom, and extorted legislative independence. The result was not, be it re-marked, a Federal union, with a Federal Government having a definite province of its own, but two independent Parliaments under one Crown; and the Crown being constitutional, the two Parliaments were two sovereign powers. There was an hourly danger of a divergence of policy, even on questions of peace and war. At the same time, the Catholics remained excluded from the Irish Parliament, and Protestant ascend-ancy was thus left rampant, without any imperial control. The consequence was that Ireland was ruled, and her policy kept in union with that of England by systematic corruption. Mr. Massey, the recent historian of this period, has found, among the original papers with which his work is enriched, a sort of chart of the Irish Parlia-ment, drawn up confidentially for the guidance of Pitt :—

"H. H., son-in-law to Lord A., and brought

into Parliament by him. Studies the law; wishes to be a Commissioner of Barracks, or in some similar place. Would go into orders, and take a living.

" H. D., brother to Lord C. Applied for office, but as no specific promise could be made, has lately voted in opposition. Easy to be had, if thought expedient. A silent, gloomy man.

" L. M., refuses to accept £500 a year : states very high pretensions for his skill in House of Commons' management. Expects £1,000 a year.—N.B. : Be careful of him.

" J. N. has been in the army, and is now on half pay : wishes a troop of dragoons, or full pay. States his pretensions to be fifteen years' service in Parliament.—N. B. : Would prefer office to military promotion ; but already has, and has long had, a pension. Character, especially on the side of truth, not favourable.

" R. P., independent, but well disposed to Government. His four sisters have pensions, and his object is a living for his brother.

" T. P., brother to Lord L., and brought in by him. A captain in the navy. Wishes for some sinecure employment."

On the government side were the members

for eighty-six proprietary seats, the owners of which had let them out for titles, offices, or pensions. Sir Arthur Wellesley, at a later period, found that a zealous supporter of the government had been endeavouring to strengthen the Union by appropriating to his own use the gold provided for the collars of the order of St. Patrick, and putting copper in its place. Meantime famine, with pestilence in its train, stalked among the Irish people, who were reduced to the level of beasts in everything except that they had the capacity of suffering as men. Does history afford a parallel to that agony of seven centuries which has not yet reached its close? But England is the favourite of heaven, and when she commits oppression it will not recoil on the oppressor.

Pitt brought in a measure of free trade with Ireland which was intended no doubt to pave the way for union. Party, combined perhaps with some real ignorance and prejudice, again led the Foxites to the side of illiberality and wrong. Their liberalism at the best was, in fact, a narrow thing. Even Burke is found on this question fighting, an Irishman against Ireland, as well as an economist against free trade.

And this time the Opposition had more than one power of evil on their side. In Ireland the jealous fears of ascendancy and jobbery were aroused. In England Protection was strong. Shall I tell it — eighty thousand Lancashire manufacturers signed a petition against free trade? All men are alike selfish, and till their selfishness is enlightened, all are protectionists. Pitt fought gallantly against this host of prejudices and cupidities. He was beaten, but his power was too strong to be shaken by the defeat.

In the article of corn, Pitt was himself a protectionist. He is taxed with apostacy by Grenville, who had studied Adam Smith with him, and who was a thoroughgoing adherent of free trade. Probably the disturbing cause in his mind was a remnant of the war theory of international policy, which assumes that each nation is a garrison, and must be ready to feed itself in case of siege. However, the case against the Corn Laws then was not so strong as it is now. There was not then the vast manufacturing and mining population which Protection afterwards compelled to live on the produce of an insufficient agricultural area, till it reached starvation prices, for the benefit of the land-lords.

But what became of Parliamentary Reform ? At the opening of his ministry Pitt still hoisted reform colours—still professed his determination to press that which, as he said, " alone could entitle Englishmen to the appellation of free, and ensure to wise, to virtuous, and to consti-tutional endeavours a victory óver factious am-bition, and corrupt venality, the great question of Parliamentary Reform." But the Reformer grew very tame in the Minister. When he did bring a measure forward it was not like his first, a liberal disfranchisement of rotten boroughs and redistribution of seats, the same which had been proposed by Chatham ; but a paltry plan for gradually buying up rotten boroughs, with the consent of the boroughmongers, and transferring the seats to counties. Even this was thrown out. The boroughmongers were shocked at the idea of treating the franchise as a matter of property to be bought or sold. The minister evidently did not put forth his power in support of the measure which consistency required him to propose ; and if he succeeded in persuading his dearest friends that his heart was in it, that only shows that his dearest friends did not always see to the bottom of his heart. It must be borne in mind, however, that when Pitt first came forward as a Parliamentary Reformer, at the close of the American war, there was great public discontent : he had made the nation contented, and now there was apathy. Yet had a good measure passed, the government and the nation alike would have felt a calm confidence in the soundness of their institutions, which would have prevented the panic dread of French infection, and saved us from the revolutionary war. This was the accepted season, and it departed, not to be recalled.

Sinecurism, as I said before, gross as it then was, Pitt scarcely attempted to attack, though with his Customs' reforms a number of useless places fell. He even goes out of his way to commend Addington for bestowing a colossal sinecure on his nephew, a boy of sixteen. Perhaps he thought corruption good enough for Addington and kept purity for himself. But the task would have been a hard one ; it might even have cost him the power which he was using, on the whole, for the public good. In the last hour of the French monarchy, when the

handwriting was on the wall, the reforming
ministers found it impossible to reduce sinecures
and pensions. The ministry of the Duke of
Wellington and Sir Robert Peel estranged Tory
support from them when they tried to save
Toryism by the same means. It is vain to
appeal to these people to give up the abuses
in order to save the system. What they care
for is not the system but the abuses.

There was one kind of corruption of which
Pitt himself was the prince. In the course of his
ministry he created or promoted in the peerage
one hundred and forty peers. The great mass
of these creations and promotions were not for
merit of any kind, but for political support. If
the Peerage of England intends, as it seemed
from the language held in the debate on life-
peerages that it did intend, to set up a divine
right against the nation, it had better not look
into its own annals : for taking those annals
from the days of Henry VIII. and his minions,
the real commencement of our present nobility
(the feudal nobility having been destroyed in
the Wars of the Roses), it would perhaps be
difficult to find a group of families whose en-
noblement had less to do with honour. The

Stuarts sold peerages for money; later peer-makers have sold them for votes. " Besides these appointments"—says Lord Stanhope, after giving an account of the accession of the Duke of Portland and his friends to Pitt's government—"beside these appointments, two or three peerages, and two or three places of less amount, gratified some less leading members of the same connection." And not only the " less leading members of the connection," who were thus gratified, but their descendants to the end of time, even though they might degenerate from the littleness of their sires, were to have a sacred and indefeasible right of legislating for a great nation. Not only so, but if they did not choose to leave their country houses or Newmarket for a division, they were to have the right of deciding by proxy the destinies of England. Is this to be classed among the anomalies which are no evils? Is not every anomaly an evil which cannot be thought of, which cannot be mentioned to a foreigner, without shame? I call this use of peerages, and I may add that of baronetcies, a kind of corruption. It is the most potent of all kinds of corruption, when the persons to be corrupted are wealthy men, wealthy upstarts perhaps, craving, as such men crave, for hereditary rank. Even the social position which a minister can partly bestow, is no small source of influence in such a community as ours. Walpole's bribery-fund was perhaps £50,000 a year: a peerage, it may be even a baronetcy, to an ambitious millionaire is worth £50,000. Therefore, it is not wealth that will keep a member of parliament entirely above corruption. The only thing that will keep him entirely above corruption is honour.

There can be no mistake as to the objects with which, in Pitt's day, the power of conferring peerages was used. " At the close of the elections," says Lord Stanhope, " the King showed his entire approval of his minister by the grant—perhaps a little lavish—of seven new peerages. The others were to baronies; but one, Sir James Lowther, whose influence at Appleby had not been forgotten, · was raised at once to higher rank, as Earl of Lonsdale." I believe it would be putting the case mildly to say that the beneficent influence of Sir James Lowther at Appleby was the only public service by which he had merited public honour. Irish peerages, of course, were granted with even a more shameful prodigality than the English, just as the Irish pension list received spies and cast-off mistresses, whose names on the English pension list would scarcely have been endured. Pitt was on the point of making a loan-contractor an Irish peer because he had parliamentary influence in England. And this is called " recruiting the peerage." So recruited, as Pym said in another great peer-making epoch, " honour itself would become a press." Perhaps Pitt was sensible of this danger, when, in framing the Regency Bill, he withheld from the Prince of Wales the power of creating peers, which would have been exercised under the advice of Fox.

Pitt's admirers plead guilty on his behalf to the charge of not patronising men of letters. But patronage of men of letters was going out of fashion, and it was happy for literature that it was so. How can a statesman have leisure to discriminate literary merit ? And if he cannot discriminate, how can we desire that he should patronise ? Of course he can be told what writers are on his own side in politics, and he can see who flatter him in their prefaces; but this is not what learning or the public wants.

A munificent despot, such as Louis XIV., may foster a Court literature : a munificent party-chief, such as the Whig leaders in the reign of Anne, may foster a party literature. A healthy literature needs no fostering but that of freedom. The best patron of intellect is an educated people.

The newspaper press was not a great power in Pitt's day. In laying a stamp duty on news-papers, he speaks of it jestingly as an interest with which the members of the House would desire to stand well. If it had been a great power, he would have deserved gratitude for not tampering with journalists. The anonymous press has done great service to reform, a service which nothing else could have done. But if its independence should ever be lost—if its great organs should ever by patronage or social in-fluence be made secretly subservient to the purposes of a dishonest minister, if its chiefs should ever forget the sacredness of their mis-sion in the " gilded saloons" of power—it would itself become the most potent and terrible, as well as the vilest, of all the engines of cor-ruption. Political evil is Protean in its forms. New diseases, new dangers arise as civilisation advances ; and the corruption of an anonymous press is by no means among the least.

The reform of the Libel Law, in the interest of liberty, received Pitt's cordial support. He was too great, at all events, to fear free criticism; though we may guess what he would have said of the use of attacks on private character as a mode of carrying on political war. Of no other law reforms was he the author. Yet he had before him a code which ought to have made any statesman a law reformer—a code truly and fearfully aristocratic—a code which, for the lower orders, was indeed written in blood—a code which, while duelling and other offences of persons of quality were practically overlooked, inflicted capital punishment with an almost unparalleled recklessness of human life on the petty offences of the poor—a code which was the proof of a deeper barbarism than the native ferocity of the untutored savage. This work was left to Mackintosh and Romilly. Unconsciously and involuntarily perhaps Pitt contributed to law reform. He put Eldon at the head of the law. And with Eldon at the head of the law, reform could no longer be delayed.

Humanity, however, honours Pitt as the

constant and powerful opponent of the slave-
trade. Perhaps he deserves in one respect to be
honoured above Wilberforce and Clarkson, inasmuch as the responsibility of the statesman is
greater than that of the private reformer. On
this question he remained true to his better
self, when on all other questions he had passed
to the side of reaction. In 1799 he carried
through the Commons a bill for the partial
abolition of the trade, which, to his great grief,
was thrown out by the Lords, on grounds which
it must be left to the advocates of hereditary
virtue to explain. His speech against the slave-
trade in 1792 is justly regarded as about his
best. A few years before, an action relating to
a policy of insurance on the value of certain
slaves had been tried in the King's Bench. The
question was, whether the loss of the slaves had
been caused by perils of the sea. A slave-ship,
with four hundred and forty-two slaves was
bound from the coast of Guinea to Jamaica.
Sixty of the slaves died on the passage from
overcrowding, but in respect of these it was not
contended that the underwriter was liable. The
captain, having missed Jamaica, found himself
short of water, and under the apprehension of

scarcity, but before his crew and passengers had been put on short allowance, he threw ninety-six of the sickliest slaves overboard. A fall of rain now gave him water for eleven days, notwithstanding which he drowned twenty-six more of the slaves. Ten in despair threw themselves overboard, for a negro is human enough to feel despair. The ship arrived in port before the water was exhausted. "Thus," says Mr. Massey, "one hundred and thirty-two human beings, if negroes are human beings, were wilfully murdered." But the city jury found that they were chattels, lost by perils of the sea, and gave £32 damages for each slave thrown overboard. The court granted a new trial on the ground that there was no such necessity for drowning the second batch of slaves as to constitute a loss by perils of the sea. There was not a thought, as Mr. Massey remarks, of proceeding against the captain or his crew for homicide. And this is a law-case of the nation which was conquering India to introduce a higher civilisation, and which justified its treatment of the Africans on the ground that they were incorrigible barbarians. One of the proofs of African barbarism adduced by the slave-traders was that a boy had been put to death by an African because a trader had refused to buy him as a slave. Pitt replies that the real reason why the boy had been put to death was that he had three times run away from his African master, who, by the native custom, had to pay his value every time he was brought back to him, and failing to dispose of him to the English slave-traders, killed him in anger, or to avoid having to pay for him again. He cites a law from the West India Statute Book, enacting that "if any negro or other slave shall withdraw himself from his master for the term of six months, or any slave that was absent shall not return within that time, it shall be adjudged felony, and every such person shall suffer death." He then bids the House compare the sudden wrath of the wild African, which slew the negro after the third offence, with the deliberate legislation of the civilised planter which puts him to death for the first, and say on which side the barbarism lies. The answer must be of course that the barbarism lies on the side which has not Enfield rifles but only bows and arrows. The slavery party of those days had not all the lights of science that the Anthropologists have now; but by the light of

their own cupidity they had discovered the
argument that the negro was by nature incapable of civilisation. Pitt asks what a Roman
senator would have said of the Britons—whether
he would not have said with confidence : "*There*
is a people that will never rise to civilisation ;
there is a people destined never to be free—a
people without the understanding necessary for
the attainment of useful arts, depressed by the
hand of nature below the level of the human
species, and created to form a supply of slaves
for the rest of the world ?"

It was deposed on the side of the slave-owners
that the middle passage was a very happy part
of the negro's life ; the air of the hold was
exactly suited to his Tropical constitution ; when
on deck he made merry and danced his national
dances. The privy Council on inquiry found
that, the better to secure the comfort of the
negroes in their Tropical hold, they were chained
two and two together or fastened by ringbolts
to the lower deck ; that they were allowed one
pint of water each daily under the line, with
two meals of yams and horse-beans ; and
that after their meals they were made to take
exercise by jumping on deck in their irons under

the lash. These were their national dances. There was one argument for the slave-trade which seems not to have been urged. The reformers did not at this time venture to propose the abolition of slavery; and, of the two, slave trading was rather better than slave breeding.

Of the Church Pitt seems to have had no conception, except as an establishment, the prizes of which were to be bestowed with some regard for piety and learning, but with a primary regard to personal and political connection. He gave Tomline a fat Bishopric and a fat Deanery at the same time. One instance Lord Stanhope has found in which he resisted the solicitation of a powerful man in order to reward a curate who had done his duty. He is disclosed to us in the life of his great friend Mr. Rose, coolly using a Deanery as a political bribe, and enjoining his agent to see that the object bargained for is secured. No thought of purifying the Church as the spiritual organ of the nation seems to have arisen in his mind. A strange spiritual organ for the nation the Church then was. Lord Stanhope has given us the following correspondence :

The Bishop of Lichfield (Dr. Cornwallis) to Mr. Pitt.

" Wimpole-street, June 10, 1791.

"Sir,—After the various instances of neglect and contempt which Lord Cornwallis and I have experienced, not only in violation of repeated assurances, but of the strongest ties, it is impossible that I should not feel the late disappointment very deeply.

" With respect to the proposal concerning Salisbury, I have no hesitation in saying that the See of Salisbury cannot be in any respect an object to me. The only arrangement which promises an accommodation in my favour is the promotion of the Bishop of Lincoln to Salisbury, which would enable you to confer the Deanery of St. Paul's upon me.

" I have the honour to be, etc.,

"J. Lichfield and Coventry."

Mr. Pitt to the Bishop of Lichfield.

" Downing-street, Saturday night, June 11, 1791.

" My Lord,—On my return to town this afternoon I found your lordship's letter. I am willing to hope that on further consideration, and recollecting all the circumstances, there are parts of that letter which you would yourself wish never to have written.

" My respect for your lordship's situation, and my regard for Lord Cornwallis, prevent my saying more than that until that letter is recalled your lordship makes any further intercourse between you and me impossible.

" I have the honour to be, etc.,

" W. Pitt."

The Bishop of Lichfield to Mr. Pitt.

"Wimpole-street, June 11, 1791.

"Sir,—Under the very great disappointment which I have felt upon the late occasion, I am much concerned that I was induced to make use of expressions in my letter to you of which I have since repented, and which upon consideration I beg leave to retract, and I hope they will make no unfavourable impression upon your mind.

"Whatever may be your thoughts regarding the subject-matter of the letter, I trust that you will have the candour to pardon those parts of it which may appear to be wanting in due and proper respect to you.

"And believe me to have the honour, etc.,

"J. LICHFIELD AND COVENTRY."

Mr. Pitt to the Bishop of Lichfield.

"Downing-street, June 12, 1791.

"My Lord,—I have this morning received the honour of your lordship's letter, dated the 11th, and have great satisfaction in being able to dismiss from my mind any impression occasioned by a paragraph in the former letter which I received from you.

"With respect to any further arrangement, I can only say that I have no reason to believe that the Bishop of Lincoln would wish to remove to Salisbury ; but, if he were, I should certainly have no hesitation in recommending your lordship for the Deanery of St. Paul's.

"I have the honour to be, etc.,

"WILLIAM PITT."

He that desireth a bishopric, desireth a good thing, but he that desireth a bishopric and a deanery together, desireth a still better thing : so, no doubt, Dr. Cornwallis would have interpreted the Scripture. And, be it observed, the covetousness of the man, his meanness, his flagrant unworthiness to hold any spiritual office, make no bad impression whatever on Pitt's mind. The only thing that makes a bad impression on his mind is the injurious expressions touching himself. When these have been retracted, he is quite ready to promote Dr. Cornwallis higher in the Church.

In another case we have an aspirant resorting to the ingenious artifice of writing to thank the minister for a blissful rumour which assigned to him a mitre then vacant. The minister has the pain of informing him that the rumour is unfounded.

Lord Stanhope gives the correspondence between Pitt and Dr. Cornwallis, with the warning that such a case could not occur now. A case so gross and palpable could not occur now. But may not things really just as bad occur now ? May not a political tactician, and one to whom regard for spiritual interests could scarcely be

ascribed except in jest, use spiritual preferment
to purchase the political support of a great religious party as cynically as ever the support of
the lords of rotton boroughs was purchased by
Pitt? May we not, in return, hear religious
adulation poured forth by Pharisaic lips to a
patron whose only title to respect, in a religious
point of view, is that he is not a Pharisee? May
we not see men who profess to be pre-eminently
Christian supporting a policy pre-eminently un-
Christian, because its author puts ecclesiastical
power into their hands? May we not see a religious connection, yesterday independent, to-day
laying down its independence and its influence
for good in the ante-chamber of a minister? May
we not see divines, the authorised guardians of
the truth, shaping their doctrine to the taste of
the great bishop-maker of the day? And if this
is so, are we really much better off now than we
were in the days of Pitt and Dr. Cornwallis?

The highest rule of duty which Pitt knew in
the use of Church patronage he kept. He was
staunch to his friends. He had high words with
the King because the King insisted on making
Moore, instead of Tomline, Archbishop of Canterbury. Tomline evidently thought that though

the country was in the midst of a great war, the
government ought to have resigned.

Whether Pitt had been at all touched by the
scepticism of his century or not, he had imbibed
its toleration.   He was always in favour of
Roman Catholic Emancipation.   He was not dis-
inclined to the repeal of the Test and Corporation Acts.   But he consulted the bishops.   It is
wonderful that of fourteen bishops two were in
favour of the repeal.   We maintain a political
hierarchy, and we must accept the natural results.   It does not lie in the mouths of Noncon-
formists, who have political power in their hands
and fail to use it for the assertion of religious
freedom, to rail at the evils of the Establishment ; for the blame of those evils rests on them.
I say it in no spirit of irony, but with sincere
conviction ; the marvellous thing in the character of the state-bishops is not the illiberality of
the many, but the liberality of the few.   Pitt's
episcopal advisers erred under the almost irre-
sistible pressure of the circumstances in which,
not their own act, but the act of the community
had placed them. Yet could they have had their
way, these questions would long ago have been
solved by civil war.   Warned by his oracles—

the keepers of the state conscience—Pitt resisted a motion for the repeal of the Test and
Corporation Acts. You can see that, like Peel
resisting Catholic Emancipation and the repeal
of the Corn Laws, he is struggling against the
dawning light within him, as well as against
the arguments from without. His reasoning is
founded on the assumption with which we are
now being made again familiar, that no man has
any political rights, and that it rests entirely
with the dominant party in the state to dole out
to their fellow citizens just as much of political
freedom and justice as they may think compatible with the ascendancy of their own opinions
and with the safety of the political arrangements
by which that ascendancy is preserved. Such
advantages as he gains are due to the weakness
of his opponents, who, though their hearts were
on the side of justice, had not yet learnt, as indeed few public men have even now learnt, to
examine boldly the duty of the state in matters
of opinion. The revolting profanation of the
sacrament, which the Test and Corporation Act
involved, as it did not shock the clergy, naturally
did not shock the man of the world.

The Commutation of Tithes into a corn-rent

was Pitt's only Church reform. It was destined mainly for Ireland. I have seen among some papers of Sir Robert Peel a picture of the levying of tithe in a Catholic's farm-yard by a Protestant parson, who is just seizing the tenth pig, while soldiers with fixed bayonets stand by to support the law. The picture is a caricature of course, but caricature itself could scarcely add deformity to the truth. Pitt, in his letter to the Lord-Lieutenant, hopes that the Irish clergy will take a sober and dispassionate view of the matter; that they will understand how much easier it is for them, by persisting in an odious system, to imperil the government than for the government to uphold them; that they will propose an accommodation, which, originating with them, would not be unbecoming. He appealed for a sober and dispassionate consideration of an angry question to men whose whole existence was a fierce conflict with a hostile nation. His plan was rejected, and he gained nothing but the credit with posterity of having been before his time.

To pass from home government to the dependencies, Pitt had thrown out the India Bill of Fox, but he could not help bringing in one of his own. The Company's servants—their cupidity inflamed to the utmost by the sight of such gorgeous booty—had burst through the frail barrier which divides the rapacious trader from the robber, and were heaping up fortunes by violence and fraud, hardly paralleled, to borrow the words of Mr. Massey, in the dark and bloody annals of conquest. Pitt was trammelled by his opposition to Fox's measure, and by his alliance with the East-India interest and the nabobs who sat for its rotten boroughs. The result was a half measure—the double government which shambled on in its awkwardness till the Sepoy Mutiny, by breaking up the army on which the dominion of the Company rested, and thus destroying one of the two powers, gave the system a final blow. The abuse of Indian patronage, the dread of which had been worked against Fox's Bill, was not avoided by that of Pitt. The corrupt dominion of Dundas in Scotland was maintained to a great extent at the expense of the Hindoo. And we soon find Lord Sydney, an honourable member of the Cabinet, complaining of the monopoly of army appointments in India by Scotchmen ; of "insatiable ambition," "sordid avarice," "base work," and "the character of men whom he had imprudently treated with great openness, but who should never come into his room again while he had a bolt to his door." Perhaps there is still something in the feelings of Scotchmen, even of pious Scotchmen, towards the oppressed people of dependencies, which savours of the old time. It may be doubted, however, whether the failure to incorporate India completely with England ought to be reckoned among the demerits of the Bill. Writers on the government of dependencies have not sufficiently considered the consequences of the relation to the character of the imperial country. The effect of incorporating a vast despotism like India with a free nation perhaps remains yet to be seen. There is a poison which is imbibed daily though it is not perceived; which was imbibed, though it was not perceived, by Imperial Spain.

In the case of Hastings, the accusers being Whigs, the Tories of course took the part of the accused, with whom, indeed, as a representative of arbitrary and sanguinary violence, they had sympathies of a more specific kind. Pitt, as is well known, turned round in the middle, and to the dismay of the mass of his party, who voted against him, carried the impeachment by the votes under his absolute command. His conversion was so mysterious that it was ascribed to jealousy of Hastings. But we may safely regard it as conscientious, and as having been delayed only by his inability to look thoroughly into the case at an earlier stage. Hastings was a great criminal, and one who, for the honour and in the highest interest of the country, ought to have been brought to justice; though he might have pleaded, in extenuation of his guilt, the evil necessities of conquest, for which his masters were more responsible than he. He was absolved, and afterwards honoured, because his crimes had served, or were supposed to have served, the aggrandisement of England. And if the aggrandisement of England is a redeeming motive before God as well as before the House of Lords, all, no doubt, will be well. Then there will be no danger of retribution, though our press, reflecting too faithfully the morality of the nation, should preach, under the thin disguise of rhetoric, doctrines which in their naked form could be avowed only in the cavern of a bandit or on the deck of a buccaneer.

Hastings and his party complained, with some

reason, of the length of a trial, conducted by a tribunal the dilatoriness of which equalled its untrustworthiness for the purposes of justice. It was about this time that a woman died in Devon County Gaol, after an imprisonment of forty-five years, for a debt of £19.

Parliament, however, displayed in the case of Hastings a higher sense of justice and of the national honour than it displays in cases of wrong done to the subject races in the present day. The conscience of the nation had not then become seared by the long exercise of empire; a perverted code of imperial morality had not had time to grow up, nor had the plea that an act was done in the interest of the dominant race yet become familiar and persuasive to English minds. On these questions we grow worse; and we shall probably continue to grow worse till for us, as for the American slave-owner, the end arrives, and we find that neither the approbation of our press, nor the acquiescence of our state-clergy, is the connivance of the Power which, after all, rules the world.

Adam Smith had proposed that the colonies should be represented in the British Parliament. Such was his cure for the conflict between imperial supremacy and colonial liberty, which was gathering to a head while he wrote. At the time, it was answered that this plan would be impracticable on account of the distance. With regard to the Australian colonies, the same objection would be fatal now. You could not, after a dissolution, wait till the returns to the writs had been made from Sidney and Melbourne, before reassembling Parliament. But the more fatal objection is that the colonies have national Parliaments of their own, and that to let them send members to the national Parliament of England also, and have a voice in our national questions, while we should have none in theirs, would involve a confusion of functions full of absurdity and injustice. If you have any common assembly for the mother country and the colonies, it must be a Federal Council, dealing with the interests of the empire apart from those of the several nations : and this Federal Council must in Federal questions be above the national government of Great Britain, an arrangement which Great Britain would never endure. A moral, commercial, and diplomatic union of all the communities of the Anglo-Saxon race, including what must soon become the greatest of those communities, the United States of America, is no dream, and if a national policy is pursued, may be made a glorious reality. But a political union of all these communities, or of those still under the nominal rule of Britain, scattered as they are over the globe, is a dream, and one from which we shall soon awake. Colonial Emancipation, while the tie of affection remains unbroken, is the only mode of securing that to which we all alike cling, that of which we all alike are proud. There is no reason why it should not be accompanied with a mutual retention of the rights of citizenship, so that an Englishman might, to all intents and purposes, be an Australian in Australia, and an Australian be an Englishman here. There is no reason why the colonies should not keep the old flag. The only thing which need be given up, and this Nature proclaims aloud must be given up, is the political dependence of a nation on one side of the globe upon a nation at the other. Towards Colonial Emancipation Pitt made the first step, still partly guided herein by his great teacher, who, though he had proposed a plan which was not feasible for the political incorporation of the

colonies with the mother couutry, had placed
their uselessness as dependencies in a clear light.
The Canadas, which had remained ours when
we lost the British Colonies in America, had
hitherto been governed as dependencies. Pitt
now gave each of them a Parliament of its own,
and thus, in fact, made them separate nations,
though to complete the severance would have
been a measure at once out of the range of his
vision, and beyond his power. The people of
French Canada being Catholics, their admission
to political rights was, in fact, Catholic Emancipation. The good King and his spiritual advisers appear to have made no objection to this
feature of the plan. Perhaps it was thought
that Providence, for commercial objects, winked
in a colony at that which it would have visited
as impiety at home. There is a beautiful plas-
ticity in our political religion. Intent on pro-
ducing another England beyond the Atlantic,
Pitt provided for the endowment of a State
Church, and for the creation of a peerage in the
colony. Ungrateful Nature has refused both
boons ; though, in the plans now framed for
Canadian Confederation, there is a proposal for
a mock House of Lords, not hereditary, but for

life, the proper materials for which the colonies, from the instability of wealth and the absence of any social distinctions there, will fail to furnish, and which, if it is set up, will, I venture to predict, in the end breed confusion. Pitt had no philosophy of history to teach him that progress is the law of things, that though the essence of religion and morality does not change, all besides is ever changing, that the scroll is not yet all unrolled, and that Providence does not mean merely to repeat itself over again in the new world. He did not know that feudalism had performed its part in the development of humanity, that of a schoolmaster, to train society for a larger freedom; that it was bound up with military aristocracy, the offspring of conquest, which with the age of conquest and military ascendancy passes away; that it was based on a tenure of land, which the English race had discarded from the moment when it set foot on the new shore. What is more, Pitt when he tried the experiment had not, like us, seen the experiment fail.

Nor is Pitt's sagacity much to be impeached because, under an unhappy star, he founded Botany Bay. Leave nature to herself and she

will choose the germs of new nations well.
Wise, beyond the reach of human wisdom, in
all her processes, she does not forget her wisdom
in this most momentous process of propagating
humanity over its destined abodes. Careful in
the selection of the right seed for a plant, she
is not careless in selecting the right colonists.
Left to herself she selects the flower of English
worth, the founders of New England; when
man undertakes to select for her, he selects the
convicts of Botany Bay, and taints the being of
future communities at its source with the pestilence of a moral lazar-house. But the severance
of the American Colonies was supposed to be a
fatal blow to the prosperity of England, which
only the foundation of new colonies could coun-
tervail, though, as we all know, it proved an immense gain, and turned the driblet of restricted
commerce into a mighty current of wealth.
Our gaols too, dens of the most hideous de-
pravity, filth, and cruelty, called loudly for
depletion, and the dream was a flattering one
of turning the felony of England into the virtue
and industry of other lands. Still mischief was
done, mischief of which the traces are not wholly
effaced yet. But I am falling into a repetition

of what I have said on the subject of colonies elsewhere.

Towards the American Colonists Chatham's son inherited the feelings of Chatham. Not only did he, as a member of the Shelburne government, gladly take part in making peace with them, but he desired in matters of trade to treat them, to the utmost of his power, as though they were Englishmen still. And they are Englishmen still, if the England, which notwithstanding all that the evil agents of a selfish faction have done to breed bitterness between us, her Colonists still love, will show that she still loves them This was treason and revolution yesterday : it is orthodoxy and Conservatism to-day.

It is said of Sir Robert Peel by a French statesman, that he had no foreign policy but peace and good-will among nations. The same thing may be said of Pitt during the first ten years of his power. He was remarkably free from the vice of diplomacy. He did not meddle except when he was called upon to do so, and then he quietly and with dignity maintained the honour of the country. It is well for the nation when the Chancellor of the Exchequer is the most powerful man in the government, because his ambition is opposed to war. The son of Chatham, while he was himself, and before he became the organ of a panic-stricken and infuriated faction, was eminently a peace minister. In 1792, while all the world was arming, he was cutting down armaments ; his army that year was only 18,000 men, and his army estimates only £1,800,000. When shall we see such estimates again ?

Once, indeed, the Minister was led into making a demonstration against the aggrandisement of Russia, in which he failed to carry the nation with him. There are politicians who would say that he stood alone in his prophetic wisdom. Probably he would at the time have succeeded in exciting the nation more if India had then been to us what it is now, and the safety of the approaches to it had been as great an object of solicitude. The Crimean war must be set down partly to the account of India ; and so must the false bent given to our diplomacy in the East, as will appear when in the question of the Eastern nationalities, Nature has asserted her power, and produced, in spite of diplomacy, Christian communities which by a more genial policy we might have made our friends. This is not the place for a discussion of the Russian peril. Mr. Massey holds the usual language on the subject : " Russia had begun to unfold those gigantic schemes of aggrandisement which modern statesmen have justly regarded as menacing the independence and civilisation of the continent with a new irruption from the northern hive." The old irruptions from the northern hive were those of nomad hordes. They were in a word not invasions but vast migrations. The modern Russians, however backward, are a settled nation, and will scarcely, like the Goths and Huns of old, put their wives and children into their waggons and descend with their herds upon the south. The Christianity which ought to restrain their lust of military aggrandisement is unhappily itself neutralised by a State Church, which, as usual, instead of being the reproving conscience, makes itself the servile organ of the passions of the Government by which it is maintained. But it is in the government, not in the Russian people, that this lust of aggrandisement resides. In this case also the beginning of political freedom will probably

be the end of military rapacity ; and, since the
emancipation of the serfs, the beginning of
political freedom can scarcely be far distant.
The fear that Europe will soon be either Republican or Cossack does not seem to me chimerical; but the fear that it will be Cossack does.

The Minister also met with a check in bringing forward a proposition, which was not his
own but the Duke of Richmond's, for the forti-
fication of the arsenals. Party came in as usual,
regardless of the safety of the country when
the paramount interest of faction was to be
served. But the feeling upon which party
played seems to have been confidence in the
sufficiency of the wooden walls. The nation
might, at all events, and may still truly say,
that Government has at its command a great
fleet, maintained at a vast expense to the
nation, and that it is bound, with this fleet,
to maintain an ascendancy in the British waters,
which if it would do, we should stand in little
need of fortifications. But the fleet is scattered
in. petty squadrons over the world, for the
nominal defence of distant colonies and dependencies, and for the hollow pretence, which
could not now be sustained six months after the

outbreak of a great war, of dominating in the Mediterranean. The country is continually pouring millions into the naval estimates, only to be told that its own shores are defenceless, and that millions more must be spent in fortifying them against French invasion.

As a member of Shelburne's government, Pitt had been called on to defend, among the other articles of the peace with America and her allies, the abandonment of the clause in the treaty of Utrecht, providing for the demolition of Dunkirk. North denounced the article, on the ground that though Dunkirk was no longer of real importance, the presence of our commissioners on the enemy's territory was to be desired, because it perpetuated the memory of former victories, exalted the dignity of Great Britain, and humbled the pride of France. Such has hitherto been the code of honour among nations. Among men true dignity is inoffensive, and he who is most careful of the honour of others is thought likely to be most careful of his own. Shelburne, like Chatham and Stanhope—two ministers of spirit as well as sense—before him, had proposed to give Gibraltar up to Spain for an equivalent. Three times round that barren rock had the waters—Nature's destined portal of peaceful commerce, and her destined highway of kindly intercourse among the nations of Christendom—been dyed with Christian blood and covered with floating agony. It does not command the entrance to the Mediterranean. It has made Spain our enemy in every war of the European Powers. When almost paralysed by decrepitude, she dragged her feeble limbs again and again to the attack, that she might remove this stain on her escutcheon, this eyesore of her honour. The recovery of it would be the greatest bribe that a military adventurer rising to power in Spain could offer to his countrymen : and perhaps the day may not be far distant when such a crisis may occur. But let us by no means exercise any foresight in the matter. Foresight is unworthy of a practical nation. A passage in one of Pitt's letters seems to indicate that he opposed Lord Shelburne on this occasion. But, if he did, it must be borne in mind that we had then no other station in the Mediterranean. Minorca had been lost : Malta was not yet ours. Pitt said " some naval station in the Mediterranean is absolutely indis-pensable, but none can be found so desirable

and secure as Malta." If we cite great authorities, we must remember the circumstances
under which they spoke. But again I am re-
peating what I have said more than once before.

In the midst of his useful course Pitt was
almost thrown out of power by the illness of
the King, which, if it had lasted longer, would
have made the 'Prince of Wales Regent, and
transferred the government to his friends ; one
of the many warnings to nations in search of a
constitution not to embrace ours without considering all the liabilities of so peculiar and
complex a machine.   The Prince of Wales,
partly from filial feeling, partly perhaps like
D'Orleans Egalitè, for the sake of another forbidden pleasure, flirted with Liberal principles,
which, however, of course, lost for ever their
place in what he was fond of calling his heart,
the instant that his foot touched the throne.
The debates on the Regency Bill, under the
guise of a great constitutional discussion, were
a scuffle for power between two factions which
had accidentlly changed their positions with
regard to royalty for the moment, and got hold
each of the other's cant ; so that if Pitt could
say that he had un-Whigged Fox, Fox might

have said that he had un-Toried Pitt. These
scenes revealed on the critical eve of the French
Revolution the scandals of Royalty—a King,
in whom the ray of reason barely flickered
swaying the destinies of a nation—the Princes
mocking at the affliction of their father—the
Queen receiving with complacency the duellist
who had nearly killed her detested child. Not
long before had occurred the episode of the
Prince of Wales and Mrs. Fitzherbert, in which
the Prince broke every law of honour, and
put up his bosom friend to tell a lie for him
in the House of Commons. But there are
extenuating circumstances in this case. First,
the Prince, like all princes, had been sacrificed
to the public good : he had never known equal
friendship, heard the voice of truth, or learnt
self-control and honour in the school of other
men. Secondly, his love for Mrs. Fitzherbert
was undoubtedly deep and sincere ; a lawful
marriage with her might have been the means
of reclaiming him. Thirdly, he had not made
the laws which, in the case of royal marriages,
sacrificed affection to policy ; and, heir to a
kingdom as he was, he might have envied the
meanest servant in his train whose hand and

heart were free. He was afterwards married to a woman whom he had never seen, and the sight of whom caused him at once to call for brandy, while further researches have revealed that he drowned the horrors of his wedding in an enormous potation of liqueur. His mother had been called down from her nursery one afternoon to dine at table with the family, and introduced to a stranger, who after dinner led her into the next room, and went through the form of marriage with her as the deputy of the King of England. When she was brought to St. James's, never having seen her destined husband, she was going to fall down at the feet of the wrong man.

The people showed their sympathy and their loyalty when the King recovered. They passed from mouth to mouth, and engraved on their rings and snuff-boxes the words of the honest Lord Chancellor Thurlow: "When I forget my King may my God forget me." They had not heard Burke's exclamation, "The best thing he can do for you," or the more pungent but highly improper comment of the graceless Wilkes; nor had they seen Pitt run out of the House crying, "Oh what a rascal." In the course of the great struggle between the King's party and that of the Prince, when the King's friends were holding a Cabinet at Windsor, as they rose to go, the honest Lord Chancellor's hat was missing. It was brought to him from the Prince's room.

And now the sun of Pitt's glory has reached its zenith. It declines towards the West and night.

PITT.—II.

IV.

P I T T. — II.

Aɴ optimist view of history will not hold good, any more than an optimist view of nature. All will be well in the sum of things, but in the meantime calamities occur. No greater calamity ever occurred, no greater disaster ever befell the cause of human progress, as it seems to me, than the revolution which brought the Liberal movement of the eighteenth century to a violent crisis in France. Apart from the faults of political character, the want of self-control, the want of mutual confidence, the levity, and worst of all the cruelty, which have marked all their revolutions, the French were from their circumstances, and from the evil training which they had undergone, quite unfit to take the political destinies of the world into their hands. The abuses of their own govern-ment were so flagrant, the obsoleteness of their

own institutions was so manifest, that the
thought of caution and moderation was banished
from their minds, and they were content with
nothing short of introducing a new order of
things, a new political creation as it were,
dating from the day of their revolt, which
they sought to extend to nations unwilling to
accept it, or unripe for a great change. They
had no middle class accustomed to government,
ready to take power into its hands, and furnish
wise rulers to the state when the aristocracy
had been overthrown. The peasantry and the
populace of their towns were brutalised to the
last degree by ignorance and oppression. The
court and the aristocracy were too utterly corrupt and effete to show any moral courage or
attempt to control the crisis which they had
themselves, by dallying with Liberalism and
Scepticism, helped to bring on; they threw
the reins on the neck of a frenzied people,
and betook themselves, for the most part, to
ignominious flight. In the whole nation, though
there were generous aspirations, there was no
faith. The state superstition had been renounced
by all men in their hearts, even by its state
supporters, even by its own priests: but its

political ascendancy had been the upas shade which had forbidden any other religion to grow. The creed of Rousseau was not a faith but an emotion, capable of impelling, not of controlling or sustaining men. Here, as Quinet in his recent work has pointed out, lay the root of the whole failure. Institutions, antiquated and decayed, may fall or be pulled down ; but humanity can advance into a new order of things only when it is borne forward on the wings of a new faith. And not a step will be made towards the attainment of a new faith by guillotining all the tyrants and oligarchs in the world.

First there was a revolutionary movement in which the generous hopes and glorious promises which fascinated the youth of Wordsworth, Southey, and Coleridge were blended with the premonitory symptoms of the crimes and horrors to come, and accompanied by an explosion of chimeras, of rhetoric, of theatrical egotism, and of political folly, the fearful significance of which is plain to the retrospective eye of history. Then ensued Anarchy and the Reign of Terror, which has left so deep and almost ineffaceable a stain on the cause of Progress, and from the effects of which that cause has suffered ever since, and is suffering to this hour. After Anarchy and the Terror came a military despotism which, by its piratical tyranny over Europe, put the hearts of all nations on the side of the national despots, who presented themselves as the only saviours from the rule of a foreign conqueror and the insolent myrmidons of his oppression. Not only George III. and his Tory ministers, not only the half-Liberal monarchy of Prussia, but an Emperor of Austria, a Bourbon King of Spain, became in the eyes of their trampled subjects liberators and friends of freedom. We are all glad that the Treaty of Vienna has been torn up; but it ought to be borne in mind that it was in its origin, partly indeed a counter-revolutionary arrangement of the despots, but partly also a military arrangement, framed, not without necessity, to secure Europe against the cruel rapacity of France. The conquests of Napoleon may have hastened the fall of feudalism, which in any case was inevitable; but what was this compared with the mischief done by the destruction of human life and of the fruits of human labour, by the reaction created in favour of the old dynasties and institutions, by the evil passions everywhere aroused, above all by the permanent impulse given to the great curse of this generation, the system of standing armies, and generally to the war spirit among nations? The Code Napoleon is vaunted as though it had sprung from the conqueror's brain and been propagated by his arms; but in fact it is merely the embodiment of the more enlightened and humane theories of jurisprudence which had been gaining ground throughout the eighteenth century, and had been to a great extent carried into effect by paternal despots, such as Leopold of Tuscany and Frederic the Great. And against the Code Napoleon we have to set the revival for the evil purposes of despotism of the state religion and the state priesthood of France.

To the Napoleonic despotism France, after a brief interlude of uncongenial freedom, has returned; and this despotism is the keystone of the system of standing armies and government by force in Europe. Like Slavery, it is inherently propagandist; and it has infected the governing class, even in this country, with a tendency to violence and martial law. Better than the Bourbon despotism it may be, inasmuch as it openly embraces social equality and religious toleration, though it covertly undermines the first by the creation of a military aristocracy, and the second by its alliance with an obscurantist and jesuitical priesthood. But if any one is inclined to take Bonapartism at its own estimate, and to concur in calling a Bonaparte a Messiah, let him first consider the progress which had been made under the forms of the old institutions by Frederic the Great, Joseph the Second, and William Pitt.

I do not wish to excuse, much less to justify, the despots of the Coalition. By their conspiracy, by their invasion of France, by the outrageous threats which, through the proclamation of the Duke of Brunswick, they uttered against the independence of the French people, they committed at once a great blunder and a great crime, and they reaped the bitter fruits of their offence. Wisdom, by the lips of old Kaunitz, had warned them of their proper course—to draw a cordon round the eruption and let the volcano consume its own entrails, as it assuredly would have done. They chose, instead of this, to tap the crater, and bring

the lava-torrent down upon themselves. Their
attack at once threw the Revolution into the
hands of the violent party, and was the proxi-
mate cause of the massacres of September and
of the Reign of Terror. It made the Revolution military. The creed of the Voltairians
was a creed of peace. Voltaire is never so
good as when he is ridiculing the cruel folly
which crimps a number of ignorant and innocent
peasants, dresses them up in uniform, teaches
them to march and wheel, and sends them off
to kill and be killed by another army of peasants, ignorant and innocent like themselves,
as a sacrifice to what is called the honour of
kings. The teachings of Rousseau were, if
possible, more pacific that those of Voltaire.
Robespierre by conviction and interest was
averse to war. And if the Girondins in their
egotism were ready, against their principles, to
invoke a war for the objects of their ambition,
the army of the Monarchy having been utterly
broken up, France was without an army, till the
advance of the Duke of Brunswick gave her
an army of despair. But we must weigh the
misdeeds even of the Coalition of Pilnitz in
a just balance. The trade of these men was

to be kings : the world, time out of mind, had sanctioned that trade : in many of the nations over which they ruled, and which were too backward for free institutions, the trade was necessary still. But the French Revolution proclaimed itself universal, and threatened all the thrones and altars of the world with change. It has been much praised for having done so, as though it had soared beyond the narrow bounds of national self-interest which limited the vision of revolutionists in other nations. Such proclamations cost no self-sacrifice ; they may spring from vanity and folly as well as from breadth of sympathy and catholicity of view ; their value must be estimated by the acts which follow ; and the acts of the proclaimers of universal brotherhood, in this instance, towards foreign nations, as well as towards each other, were unhappily the acts of brothers Cain. Those who were the first to welcome them with open arms were the first to feel their rapacity and insolence. But, at all events, the announcement of universal revolution could not fail to arouse the instinct of self-preservation in established governments, and such a combination as the Coalition of

Pilnitz was morally certain to result. Neither the English Revolution of the seventeenth century nor the American Revolution proclaimed itself universal; both of them entered at once into friendly relations with other governments of whatever form; yet these revolutions did more in the end than the French Revolution for the liberties of mankind.

We may be thankful, at all events, that the fortunes of humanity, in this its critical transition from feudalism to the era of equality and justice, are now partly placed in other hands; and that from the extinct volcano of Jacobinism we may turn to a United Italy and a United Germany, unsullied by terrorism and full of hope.

There can be no sadder proof of the bad effects of the French Revolution on the general interest of Progress than the conversion of Pitt to the side of the Reaction. He was as far as possible from wishing to attack the revolution. Probably he sympathised with it while it kept terms with reason and humanity. He had entered into the most friendly relations with the American Republic, notwithstanding the influence of the American Revolution on

Ireland. In 1792, when violence had already begun in France, he reduced his army, struck off two thousand seamen, and held out the highest hopes of further relief from taxes within the next fifteen years. " For although," said he, in his budget-speech, " we must not count with certainty on the continuance of our present prosperity during such an interval, yet un-questionably there never was a time in the history of this country when, from the situation of Europe, we might more reasonably expect fifteen years of peace than we may at the present moment." He looked forward to the abolition of Customs' duties, which would have been at the same time the inauguration of free trade. All his plans and hopes were bound up with peace. He stood aloof from the Congress of Pilnitz. Had his action been free, he would probably have stood aloof to the end.

The fears and passions of the Court, the aristocracy, and the clergy, had, however, been aroused ; the progress of the revolution daily increased the excitement among these classes, and it was raised to the highest pitch by the declamations of Burke. As an economical and Indian reformer, Burke, in the earlier part of

his career, had been one of the best organs of
the movement, into the reaction against which
he now flung himself headlong. If the greatness
of offences were to be measured, not by the
badness of the intention, but by the badness
of the effect, few greater offences would ever
have been committed than the publication of
the "Reflections on the French Revolution."
It was the special duty of a political philoso-
pher at that moment to allay passion, to bring
the nation under the dominion of its reason, and
to enable it to meet calmly and wisely the
tremendous crisis through which Europe was
evidently about to pass. Mr. Buckle thinks
that Burke, who up to this time had been the
first of statesmen, now suddenly went mad.
But the truth is, that two of his best treatises,
the "Letter to Sir Hercules Langrishe" and
the "Thoughts on Scarcity," were written after
the "Reflections on the French Revolution."
In a certain sense he had always been mad ; his
reason had always been liable to be overpowered
by his imagination ; he had always in his
moments of passion been incapable of self-
control ; he had always had in him that which
is commonly the root of madness, for he was a

great egotist, and his egotism is always breaking
out under the thin disguise of an affected self-
depreciation. He had lost the ear of the House of
Commons as much by his extravagance and rant
as by his prolixity ; he had come to be regarded
not only as a dinner-bell but as a fool ; and if
we are scandalised at the exclusion of this man
of genius from the Cabinet, people in 1789
would have been more scandalised at his admission. "Folly personified," he was called by one who
had just been hearing his speech on the Regency
Bill ; and the same witness says that he finished
his wild speech in a manner next to madness.
When the house would not listen to his ravings,
he called them a pack of hounds. He described
the Lord Chancellor as a man with black brows
and a large wig, and said he was fit to do an act
worse than highway robbery. He spoke in
offensive language even of the afflicted King.
He called upon the Clerk to read the Great
Charter because a bill for the reduction of offices
trenched on some vested interests. He took a
dagger out of his pocket, and hurled it on the
floor of the House, as a symbol of the atrocity
of the French Revolution ; upon which Sheridan
remarked that he had brought the knife, but he

had forgotten to bring the fork. He deserves
the national gratitude for having summoned
Hastings before the bar of justice ; but the violence of his sallies in the course of the trial
gave a great advantage to the accused. Though
he was by principle a free trader, his party
passions had led him to oppose Pitt's measure
for free trade with Ireland. He was now discredited, somewhat neglected by his friends,
restless from mortified self-love, and ready for
an outbreak. Mad in any other sense he was
not.

No doubt in the "Reflections" he is sincere. He was a worshipper of Constitutional
Monarchy. It was his Fetish. He loved and
adored it with the passionate loyalty which, as
an Irishman in his own country, he would have
felt towards the chief of his clan. Politics were
his religion, to which, in his mind, any other
religion was subservient, as he showed, when
for political purposes, he supported the imposi-
tion of the Thirty-Nine Articles on the reluctant
consciences of clergymen who had petitioned for
relief. His philosophy afforded no firm and
lofty ground of immutable faith in things unseen, from which he could form a rational

estimate of political systems, as things merely
subservient to the higher life of man, venerable
only for their utility, not to be altered without
good reason, but when there was good reason, to
be altered or abolished without superstitious scru-
ple, and destined like all other parts of the outward vesture of humanity to pass away before the
end. He did not know that, while many things
that are of man are good, nothing is sacred but
that which is of God. He was not so much an
advocate as a priest of the constitution and its
mythical founders; he preached sermons on it
as fervent as those of Bossuet, and defended its
absurdities by arguments which his piety suggested as strange as ever a Roman friar used in
defence of his superstitions. According to him
it was ordered by a sort of divine wisdom that
Cornwall should have as many members as
Scotland, because the representation was thus
prevented from being too closely connected with
local interests. When the French Revolution
got beyond his consecrated type, it forfeited his
sympathies, and with a nature so passionate as
his, to forfeit sympathy was to incur hatred.

I do not complain of his strictures on the
folly and incompetence of the French Revo-

lutionists. Here he could scarcely go beyond
the truth. But I complain of his blindness,
which charity, making the utmost allowance
for the frenzy of rhetoric, can scarcely pronounce
altogether involuntary, to the evils of the French
Monarchy and Church—I should rather say his
raving panegyrics on things shocking to sense
and virtue. "Ideas furnished from the ward-
robe of a moral imagination"—"decent drapery
of life"—"vice losing half its evil by losing all
its grossness"—is it possible that he can sincerely have applied such terms to the system
of Louis XV., of the Regent Orleans, of Cardinal Dubois? Knowing, as he must have done,
the character of the French aristocracy, can he
in perfect good faith have uttered in relation to
them the blasphemous extravagance that there
were two sources of all good in Europe, the
spirit of religion and the spirit of a gentleman?
Knowing, as he must have done, the condition of
the French people, and the responsibility of the
Court for their misery, can he have failed to be
aware of the sophism of which he was guilty in
presenting that Court under the image of the
Dauphiness as a star rising full of beauty and
beneficence over the horizon of Versailles? That

this beautiful and beneficent monarchy was bankrupt is a fact of which its devotee just shows himself conscious, and the remedy suggested by the great public moralist is in effect robbery of the public creditor, which he thinks preferable to any appropriation of the property of the State Church. He defends the ecclesiastical sinecurism so enormous in France, on the ground that ecclesiastics make as good a use of property as laymen ; an argument which would prove that there can scarcely be too much corruption in the Church. His political philosophy does not enable him, in his anti-revolutionary transports, to distinguish between the character of feudalism in its own day and its character when its day was past, or between the situation and the difficulties of the English nation in 1688 and those of the French people in 1789. In this vituperation of the National Assembly and the movement party in France, if he is sometimes telling, he sometimes sinks to the level of a scold. His declamations against declaimers, his sophistical attacks upon sophisters, the contempt which he the economical reformer affects for economists and calculators, would move a smile if we did not know how

terrible their effect had been. He talks unc-
tuously of religion, and lashes himself and his
readers into fury against French Atheism. Soon
we find him at the feet of Catherine of Russia,
a Voltairian in creed, and more than a Voltairian
in practice, conjuring her, with fulsome flattery,
to lend the aid of her unscrupulous arms in
crushing the objects of his political aversion.
Burke broke with his old party: he won the
affection, almost the worship, of a new party,
the fierce applause of a new audience. He
received a pension, and the promise of a peerage,
from the Court and the Tory Government. His
eminence entitled him to a pension if anybody
was to be pensioned, and to a peerage if he, a
peer of intellect, cared to be a lord. But that
he should accept these rewards of his change of
party was another proof of the truth of his own
statement—that the age of chivalry was gone.

Of course the clergy were deeply moved, and
the drum ecclesiastic beat to arms. Horsley,
the leading political bishop of the day, and a
sort of ecclesiastical henchman of Pitt, is known
as the author of the maxim " that the people
have nothing to do with the laws but to
obey them." This prelate preached a sermon,

published in his works, in which, correcting the imperfect views of the Founder of Christianity, he lays it down that a conscientious submission to the sovereign power is, *no less* than brotherly love, a distinctive badge of Christ's disciples— in other words, that the distinctive badge of Christians is to love one another and be Tories. He thanks God that in the Church of England both these marks of genuine Christianity have ever been conspicuous. He then proceeds to say ' that in the exercise of brotherly love, it is perhaps the amiable infirmity of Englishmen to be too easy in admitting the claim of a spiritual kindred—that the times compel him to remark that brotherly love embraces only brethren—that the term of holy brotherhood is profaned by an indiscriminate application—that if persons living under the British constitution have dared to exult in the proceedings of the French revolutionists, with them it is meet that we abjure all brotherhood ; a claim on our charity these miserable men may have, they have none on our brotherly affection.' If this was preached by a man of sense and learning in a responsible position and before an intelligent audience, we may imagine what was preached

from the rural pulpit before the squire. It is
to be borne in mind, however, that if the State
bishops and clergy, who supposed their wealth
and their privileges to be in danger, inveighed
against the impiety of revolution, so did Robert
Hall, fascinated as he had been at first by its
political promises and hopes. The French atheists
shocked all decency, as well as all religion.

It must be added that Fox behaved unwisely.
His generous heart was on the side of liberty :
but there was too much in him of the Palais
Royal, too much of the former member of the
gambling club at Almack's, where people played
for desperate stakes, with masks to conceal their
emotions and a wild masquerading dress to
typify their delirious excitement. The political
arena was to him still a gambling-table : and
his strong point was not self-control. He ought,
in the interest of his cause, to have repressed the
ardour of his sympathies, to have blamed the
excesses while he showed the benefits of the
Revolution, to have pointed out how inevitable
it was in France, how different was the case of
the English from that of the French Monarchy,
how small was the danger in England of French
contagion ; and then to have insisted that for

whatever danger there might be, the right antidote was not war or violent repression, but
timely measures of reform.   He would thus have
strengthened the hands of Pitt, whom he must
have known to be moderate, in resisting the war
tendencies of his party and of the Court.   Instead
of this he held the language of a Jacobin, and
at once inflamed the panic and wounded the
national pride by talking of the Revolution as
the most glorious event since Saratoga and York-
town.   His hot-headed followers, of course, went
beyond their chief.   But he was the leader of
the Opposition, and the function of a leader of
Opposition is, at all costs and hazards, to assail
and to embarrass the Government.   Whilst this
system of party government lasts it must be so.
But we will hope that party government is not
to be the end of all things ; and that in the
course of our political changes we shall find a
way of establishing a Government to which we
may all feel loyal, and which we may all desire
to support as the Government, not of a party,
but of the nation.

For one of his speeches Fox has been rather
unreasonably blamed. Speaking of the refusal
of the French guards to act against the people,

he said that the example˄ of a neighbouring
nation had proved the fear of standing armies
to be unfounded, since it was now shown that
by becoming a soldier, a man did not cease to
be a citizen. This, at the time, brought on a
storm of denunciation, which still rebellows in
the histories. "All the objections," says Mr.
Massey, "that have been urged by theoretical
writers and popular orators against permanent
military establishments, sink into insignificance
when compared with the appalling magnitude
of the danger attendant on an armed force which
is to arbitrate in disputes or conflicts between
the people and their rulers." Mr. Massey fails
to see that, as it is, the armed force in the hands
of the rulers all over Europe arbitrates in the
disputes and conflicts between the rulers and
the people. Standing armies are the bane of
the world, and to make them a perfect curse it
is only necessary to extinguish in the soldier
the last spark of the citizen and the man.
Soldiers, while they are soldiers, must submit
to a rigid discipline, and move at the word of
command: it is the condition of their calling and
the dictate of their honour. But I claim for the
soldier, whether officer or private, the rights of

labour and of man. I claim for him, in the first place, the right to dispose, like other men, of his own industry; to make the best terms he can for himself, like other men, in the labour market, and to give his employer warning—such warning, of course, as the nature of the calling may reasonably require—if fair terms are not allowed. In this way our army might be smaller, but it would be better than it is now. In the second place, I claim for the soldier the right to retire, and to deliver up his arms, though by no means to use them against his employer, when he finds that his military duties are likely to come into conflict with his duties as a citizen. There will be no fear of his exercising this right, unless the heart of the nation is really against the Government, and when the heart of the nation is really against the Government, the Government ought not, if politics are a matter of reason and justice, to have the means of putting down the nation by brute force. The habit of treating the soldier for a long term of years as the bondman of the Government and the blind instrument of its will, is a relic of barbarism, against which advancing civilisation will in the end protest.

Pressed by his own party, not supported in his resistance by the Opposition, Pitt, though the spirit of Adam Smith struggled hard and long in him, began to slide towards war. He first showed his tendency by a royal proclamation against seditious writings, and by measures of half hostility towards France—an Alien Bill pointed against French emissaries, an Act prohibiting the circulation of assignats, and another prohibiting the exportation of corn and flour to France. At last he himself caught, or affected to catch, the panic, and held wild language about his head being in danger. The French Republicans meanwhile, by their aggressive violence and their frantic language, were giving every possible handle to their enemies. To treat their wild propagandism, their decrees of universal revolution, as the ravings of madmen, whose paroxysm would soon be over, and who would too surely avenge their outrages on themselves, was the course pointed out by wisdom : but it was not an easy course for Pitt to take The execution of the king—a proceeding as disgusting in its theatrical levity, as it was shocking in its cruelty—gave a deathblow to the hope of peace. The French ambassador was ordered to leave the kingdom, and there was war. My belief is that Pitt felt he was doing wrong : but though a patriot and a man of honour, he had not a god in his breast. He could not resign power and break with all his friends. Reasoning like a financier, and seeing the depreciation of the French assignats, he thought that it would be a short war. When he found himself deceived in this, he made earnest, even humiliating efforts, to negotiate, to buy, a peace.

And what was the cause of this war which suspended all political and social progress for thirty years, or rather threw it back to a point which it had reached early in the eighteenth century, and under the fiscal burdens of which, and its perhaps still heavier burdens of other kinds, we still groan ? Established morality permits statesmen to resort to arms without having first tried arbitration, and this in cases where their personal prejudices or rivalries may be the real obstacles to a pacific settlement. But they are bound to assign a definite ground of war, without which there can be no assignable terms of peace. In the case before us no definite ground of war has been assigned down to the present day. From the various authorities on the subject, you would gather that England took up arms to put down the Jacobins, to save herself from the contagion of revolutionary principles, to punish regicide, to check the territorial aggrandisement of France, to establish the existence of the Supreme Being, and to close the navigation of the Scheldt.

To have gone to war for the purpose of closing the Scheldt would have been the act of a greater maniac than the Jacobins. It would have been like fighting about a right of way in the middle of an earthquake. But the truth was that we were concerned in the matter only as guarantors, and the Dutch did not call upon us to perform our guarantee.

As Burke wrote against a Regicide peace, he must have looked upon the execution of the King as the ground of the war. The murder of the French King was an offence against heaven, and heaven would certainly have visited it, and did visit it, though not by the thunderbolt, by a sure moral retribution, as well as the still more dastardly and atrocious murder of the Queen, upon the savages by whom it was committed. But it was no offence against us. In was in fact committed partly in imitation of our execution of Charles I. And if the murder of the King was the cause of the war, what was to be its object? To bring the King to life again? Or to punish his murderers? Or to punish the whole French nation? If there was to be no Regicide peace, how was a war with Regicides to be brought to an end?

The vindication of public right is another ground assigned for the war. The conduct of the French Republicans to the countries which they overran was infamous. But they had violated no public right which we were concerned to defend. The allied kings had attacked them; they had beaten the allied kings, taken the offensive, and commenced a career of conquest in their turn. This was the fortune of war. And these allies of ours in the cause of public right, what sort of champions of that cause were they? Austria, Prussia, and Russia had just consummated the partition of Poland, the most flagrant violation of public right in history, and one against which, let them roll as many stones to the mouth of that sepulchre as they will, nature and justice will protest till right is done. Not only so, but when we had become

their confederates, Austria and Prussia took
possession by robbers' law of Condè and Valen-
ciennes, in spite of the protest of the Bourbons,
for whom, as legitimate sovereigns of France,
the allies professed to fight; and when Austria
afterwards, in concert with Bonaparte, committed
an act of brigandage by the seizure of Venice,
this produced in us no moral repugnance to
her alliance. The conduct of England was, as
I am prepared to maintain, more disinterested
on the whole, as well as marked by greater
constancy and fortitude than that of any other
nation engaged on either side. Her liberties,
imperfect as they were, breathed into her government a spirit of honour which was not found
elsewhere, and checked infamies which in the
secret counsels of despotism were conceived without shame and perpetrated without rebuke. But
even England from the beginning made it a
war of interest as well as of alleged principle;
and our first act was the appropriation of the
Island of Tobago.

French propagandism, and especially the
propagandist decree of the 19th November,
1792, is another alleged justification of the war.
But this was merely the counterblast to the

propagandism of the Duke of Brunswick. If it was lawful for the allies to declare themselves the protectors of Monarchy in France, it was equally lawful for the French to declare themselves the protectors of Republicanism in other countries. We ourselves avowed, though with faltering accents, that it was part of our object to change the government of France. The decree of the 19th November, so far as we were concerned, was empty fanfaronade; no execution could be had of it in this country provided our government behaved decently to our people; it might have been treated by England as the insult of a lunatic, which touches no man's honour.

Was it against French Atheism that we went to war? This probably was the leading motive of the clergy. It cannot have been the motive of Pitt. He at least must have had sense enough to know that mankind could not be convinced of the existence of a beneficent Creator by filling creation with blood and havoc. And who were the representatives of religion? An Emperor of Austria, who shortened his life by self-indulgence; a King of Prussia, of whom it was said, in allusion to his emulation of Frederic the Great, "that he had nothing of Solomon but his concubines;" the Semiramis of the North; Prince-Bishops of the Rhine, whose petty courts were noted as the sacred scenes of every pleasure. Among ourselves, the Duke of York with his Nancy Parsons; Lord Chancellor Thurlow, who died with the name of God on his lips, but not in prayer; not to mention the Minister himself, who sometimes saw two speakers instead of one.

The great Tory authority, Sir Archibald Alison, is very frank and explicit. He says that what the Government had in view was not the conquest of the Republicans, but a danger nearer home : that they dreaded domestic revolution if pacific intercourse were any longer carried on with France. He cites a remark of the Empress Catherine to the effect that war is sometimes the only way of giving a useful direction to the passions, and says that in this remark is to be found the true explanation and the best vindication of the French war. "The passions," he proceeds, "were excited, democratic ambition was awakened; the desire of power, under the name of reform, was rapidly gaining ground among the middle ranks, and the institutions of the country were threatened

s

with an overthrow as violent as that which had recently taken place in the French Monarchy. In these circumstances the only mode of checking the evil was by engaging in a foreign contest, by drawing off the ardent spirits into active service, and in lieu of the modern desire for innovation, rousing the ancient gallantry of the British people." Sir Archibald is certainly wrong as to the fact. The institutions of the country were not threatened with overthrow. The people were loyal; they had shown the utmost enthusiasm on the recovery of the King's health. Burke himself said that not one man in a hundred was a Revolutionist. Fox's revolutionary sentiments met with no response, but with general reprobation, and caused even his friends to shrink from his side. Of the so-called Jacobin Societies, the Society for Constitutional Information numbered only a few hundred members, who, though they held extreme opinions, were headed by men of character, and were quite incapable of treason or violence. The Corresponding Society was of a more sinister character; but its numbers were computed only at 6,000, and it was swallowed up in the loyal masses of the people.

The mob at Birmingham rose for Church and
King, and sacked the house of Priestley because
he was an Atheist, or, what was the same thing,
a man of science. A Tory mob at Manchester
treated Mr. Walker, a respectable Reformer of
the place, in a similar manner. We had a
Parliament of rotten boroughs, but still a Parliament; a law framed more in the interest of
the rich than of the poor, but still a law; a
free press; trial by jury and Habeas Corpus,
no lettres de cachet, no Bastille. The State
Church was unjustly privileged, but not persecuting; and the Dissenters, if they did not
love the Test and Corporation Acts, had no
desire to worship the Goddess of Reason in
the form of a naked prostitute on the altar
of St. Paul's. The religious middle classes were
soon repelled by the impieties of the Revolution,
social enthusiasts like Coleridge and Southey
by its atrocities, all men of sense by its mon-
keyism and its madness. Foreign emissaries can
do nothing except where there is widespread
disaffection among the people. The army, navy,
yeomanry, and militia were perfectly sound.
Volunteers in large numbers answered the call
of the Government. At the threat of a French

invasion the nation would have risen as it had risen against the Armada. In Ireland alone there was real and just hatred of the Government: but the long pressure of an iron tyranny had crushed Ireland into mute despair: and in this case, as in all cases, Irish disaffection was rendered dangerous only by the war which brought it the aid of foreign arms. The Government had but to rule well, tread steadily in the path of moderate reform, and keep the defences in good order. England would then have passed unscathed through the crisis, and the wisdom of her rulers would have ensured the gratitude of the nation. But supposing that the reverse had been the case: supposing that the Tory panic had been as well founded as it was groundless;—does the morality of Sir Archibald Alison and his party sanction the maxim of the virtuous Catherine, that governments are at liberty to divert troublesome aspirations into the channel of a foreign war? Is there anything more dangerous than this in the ravings of the Jacobins? Is there anything more immoral in Machiavelli? The principle, no doubt, is intended for the exclusive use of such governments as Tories desire to uphold. But its application cannot be arrested there. If the Tories had a right to divert revolutionary sentiment into the channel of war, the Jacobins had a right to divert reactionary sentiment into the same channel : and Napoleon had the same right to get rid in the same manner of the sentiments which, as he declared, threatened the stability of his throne.

The same remark applies to the excuse founded on the danger of political contagion. Are all governments to be alike licensed to make war with their neighbours for the purpose of political quarantine ? Is the privilege to be extended to republics disquieted by the neighbourhood of monarchies and aristocracies, as well as to monarchies and aristocracies disquieted by the neighbourhood of republics ? Or is it taken for granted that no free commonwealth can be so ill-rooted in the affection of its citizens, or so wicked as to make use of such a power ?

It is sad to say it, but when Pitt had once left the path of right, he fell headlong into evil. To gratify the ignoble fears and passions of his party, he commenced a series of attacks on English liberty of speaking and writing, which Mr. Massey, a strong anti-revolutionist, characterises as unparalleled since the time of Charles I. The country was filled with spies. A band of the most infamous informers was called into activity by the Government. Men were prosecuted for loose or drunken words, of which no man of sense would have taken notice, and for speculative opinions with which no Government had a right to interfere. An attorney, named Frost, for saying in a coffee-house, where he could not have intended to conspire, and out of which he was, in fact, kicked by the company, that he was for equality and no king, was tried before Lord Kenyon, a high Tory judge, and sentenced to six months' imprisonment, to stand in the pillory, to find security for good behaviour, and to be struck off the roll. The courts of quarter session, with their benches of Tory squires, were employed to try political cases by the Government, to which their character as tribunals must have been too well known. Associations were formed under Government patronage, for the detection and prosecution of sedition, and thus the impartiality of the jury was tainted at its source. There was a Tory reign of terror, to which a slight increase of the panic among the upper classes would probably have lent a redder hue.

Among other measures of repression the Habeas Corpus Act was suspended ; and the liberties of all men were thus placed at the mercy of the party' in power. The Habeas Corpus Act is an Act of Parliament which Parliament may suspend. But the security of all English freemen from arbitrary arrest, as well as from any punishment without a trial by their peers, rests not on the Habeas Corpus Act, but on the great clause of the Great Charter, of which the Habeas Corpus Act is merely a supplement and guarantee. And the Great Charter is not an Act of Parliament: it is a fundamental covenant between the Government and all the people of these realms, a covenant which was before Parliament, which is above Parliament, and with which if Parliament tampers, it may continue to reign by force, but it will no longer reign by right. The tyranny of the Crown is past : it is the tyranny of the House of Commons against which we have now to guard. A House of Commons, not the prerogative of the Crown, was Pitt's instrument in his aggressions upon public liberty. "I called a Parliament in Ireland," was the plea of Strafford, when he was accused of arbitrary government. "Parliaments without parliamentary liberties," replied Pym, "are but a fair and plausible way to servitude." A class Parliament is an oligarchy with a broad basis, more powerful for iniquity than any Crown.

In the cases of Horne Tooke and his associates, the Government well knew that there was no real evidence of treason. The charge of constructive treason was brought in instead of that of sedition, to make an impression on the nation and possess the public mind with the idea that there were terrible conspiracies on foot. But to bring men to trial for their lives for such a purpose was a profanation of the courts of justice. The constructive treason was made out thus : 'The prisoners had issued a prospectus for a convention. To issue a prospectus for a convention was to enter into a conspiracy to compel the King to govern otherwise than by the laws. A conspiracy to compel the King to govern otherwise than by the laws was a conspiracy to depose him from the royal state, title, power, and government. Such an attempt must lead to resistance. Resistance must lead to the deposition of the King, and his deposition must endanger his life.' Such was the substance of the capital indictment which it took the Attorney-General nine hours to state. Supposing that policy could ever find a place in the proceedings of public justice, no sound policy could lead the Government to incur an ignominious defeat. Sir Archibald Alison says the trials did good, because the acquittal of the prisoners showed the public that liberty was not on the decline, and the people, satisfied with this great victory over their supposed oppressors, relapsed into their ancient loyalty. A profound way of attaching the people to the Government—to exhibit it to them as a tyrannical aggressor defeated in an attempt to wrest law to the purposes of judicial murder!

It was in one of these state trials, where the accused, Major Cartwright, was the leader of a Parliamentary Reform Association, that the Pitt of former days, the Pitt who had once been a member of the same association and the foremost champion of its principles, was put into the witness-box by the defence to bear witness against Pitt the renegade from Reform, the persecutor of Reformers in these evil times. Pitt might plead that circumstances were altered, and that when circumstances are altered, honourable men may change. Honourable men may change, and that they should have full liberty of change is essential to the public interest and to the integrity of public life. But no great nature ever passes a sponge over its former self : no great nature ever persecutes old friends.

It was in one of these trials, too, that Eldon, then Sir John Scott and Attorney-General, opened his attempt to procure the capital conviction of a man who he knew had done nothing worthy of death with a pathetic exordium on his own disinterestedness and virtue. "He should have nothing to leave his children but his good name." And then he wept. The Solicitor-General wept with his weeping chief. "What is the *Solicitor* weeping for ?" said one bystander to another. "He is weeping to think how very little the Attorney will have to leave his children."

The juries at quarter sessions of course gave

the verdicts desired by their proprietors on
the bench. The London juries on the whole
behaved well, and deserve our gratitude for
their guardianship of public liberty in its
hour of trial. They had not then been so
entirely relieved of apprehension for their own
liberties as to make them regardless of the
liberties of others. The judges behaved not
so well. The tenure of the judges is independent. But after all they belong to a
political party, and they belong to a social
class; and these are influences which, even
on the judgment-seat, only the highest and
strongest natures can entirely put aside. How
to appoint judges who shall be strictly impartial in political cases, is, I fear, a problem
still to be solved. But the judge who does
in political cases show himself above everything
but justice is one of the greatest and noblest
benefactors of his kind; he presents law in
its highest majesty to the reverence of the
people; and extinguishes in the hearts of
men the sources of violence and revolution.

In Scotland the Tory reign of terror was
worse than in England. In Scotland there
was scarcely the mockery of a representation

of the people. The entire electoral body was
not more than four thousand. Edinburgh and
Glasgow had each a constituency of thirty-three
electors. The county of Bute had one resident
elector, who constituted the meeting, called
over the freeholders, answered to his own
name, moved and seconded his own nomination,
put the question to the meeting, and unanimously elected himself. Every county and
borough was in the hands of some proprietor.
The whole country was one nest of jobbery
and corruption, managed in the interest of
the Tories, or I suppose we must say of
religion and the Supreme Being, by that
eminent servant of Heaven, Mr. Dundas. The
juries partook of the general slavishness, the
judges were fiercer Tories than the judges in
England, and much less honest. Thomas Muir,
a young advocate of high talents and attain-
ments, was an active champion of parliamentary
reform, as any man in Scotland who had
not the spirit of a serf would have been,
and had been a delegate to the Edinburgh
convention of Associated Friends of the People.
An indictment for sedition was preferred against
him by the Government. "Every incident

of the trial," says Sir Erskine May, the author
of the "Constitutional History of England,"
"marked the unfairness and the cruel spirit
of his judges. In deciding on the relevancy
of the indictment, they dilated upon the enor-
mity of the offences charged, which in their
judgment amounted almost to high treason, the
excellence of our constitution, and the terrors
of the French Revolution. It was plain that
any attempt to amend our institutions was in
their eyes a crime. All the jurymen, selected
by the sheriff and picked by the presiding
judge, were members of an association at
Goldsmiths' Hall, who had erased Muir's name
from their books as an enemy to the constitution. He objected that such men had
already prejudged his cause; but he was
told that he might as well object to his
judges, who had sworn to maintain the constitution. The witnesses for the Crown failed
to prove any seditious speeches, while they
all bore testimony to the earnestness with
which Muir had counselled order and obedience to the law. Throughout the trial he
was browbeaten and threatened by the judges.
A contemptible witness against him was caressed

by the public prosecutor, and complimented
by the court; while a witness for the defence
was hastily committed for concealing the truth,
and Muir, when he offered to speak on his
witness's behalf, was silenced and told that
he had no right to interfere in the business.
In the spirit of a bygone age of judicature
the Lord Advocate denounced Muir as a de-
mon of sedition and mischief. He even urged
it as a proof of guilt that a letter had been
found among his papers addressed to Mr. Fyshe
Palmer, who was about to be tried for sedition."
Let us hope that the age of judicature, when
a dominant party in possession of party courts
of justice, or of those still more convenient
instruments, courts of martial law, could murder
the objects of its political hatred under the form
of a trial, is as completely bygone as Sir
Erskine May imagines. Scroggs and Jeffreys
are in their graves of infamy; but their spirit
is not quite dead. Muir defended himself
gallantly, and drew from the audience applause,
which one of the judges noticed as a proof
of the seditious feelings of the people. He
asserted that he was brought to trial for
promoting parliamentary reform. "The Lord

Justice-Clerk Braxfield," remarks Sir Erskine May, " confirmed this assertion by charging the jury that to preach the necessity of reform at a time of excitement was seditious." The judge harangued the jury against parliamentary reform. " The landed interest," he said, " alone had a right to be represented; as for the rabble who had nothing but personal property, what hold had the nation on them ?" Another judge said, " If punishment adequate to the crime of sedition were to be sought for, it could not be found in our law, now that torture was happily abolished." Torture is not abolished, if the theories now maintained by servile lawyers and prerogative politicians on the subject of martial law be true : if these theories be true, English freemen are still liable to torture. Muir was sentenced to transportation for fourteen years. " Of the three Roman punishments, crucifixion, expo- sure to wild beasts, and deportation," said one of the judges, " we have chosen the mildest." Chosen the mildest he had not, but a people not so barbarous as its rulers had forced him to take it. In another trial, a judge said, in summing up to the jury, " Gentlemen, the right of universal suffrage the subjects of this country never enjoyed; and were they to enjoy it, they would not long enjoy either liberty or a free constitution. You will therefore consider whether telling the people that they have a just right to what would unquestionably be tantamount to a total subversion of the constitution, is such a writing as any person is entitled to compose, to print, and to publish." Under such law, delivered from the bench of justice, a man was condemned to transportation for seven years. If, as Pym said, parliaments without parliamentary liberties are but a fair and plausible way to servitude, jury trial without impartial judges and honest juries is but a fair and plausible way to murder.

Was Pitt answerable for all this? He was. With full knowledge of the facts he defended these outrages and their perpetrators in Parliament. The infamy cannot be wiped away from his once pure and patriotic name. Lord Stanhope pleads that these and still more violent measures were demanded by the temper of the time. Does not the very fact, that the temper of the time was what Lord Stanhope

states it to have been, prove that there was
no danger of revolution, and therefore not
even that wretched justification for these outrages on liberty and law? And if the demand
of a party was a warrant for violence in the
case of the Tories, was it also a warrant for
violence in the case of the Jacobins? It seems
that Pitt even sank so far below his nobler
self as to entertain the thought of taking advantage of the free language of his rival, Fox,
and committing him to the Tower.

The worst Reign of Terror, however — a
Reign of Terror in no figurative sense — was
in Ireland. Unhappy Ireland, and still more
unhappy England if Ireland is always to be
our weakness and our shame, the standing
confutation alike of our boasted statesmanship
and of our boasted love of justice! In 1795,
the Duke of Portland and the Whig section
of the Cabinet, I fear against the wishes of
Pitt, had sent over Lord Fitzwilliam as Lord-
Lieutenant, with a policy of relief and conciliation. But Fitzwilliam had been too open
in proclaiming his mission; he had been too
hasty in setting his heel on the agents of
tyranny and corruption; most fatal error of

T

all, he had dismissed one of the great robber house of Beresford. The whole nest of jobbers were immediately alarmed; and as the means of arresting justice they naturally had recourse to religion. They appealed against Catholic Relief to the conscience of the King. We are frail beings, but conscience is always obeyed when she bids us deny a right to others. Fitz-william fell; not, it is to be feared, to the displeasure of Pitt, and was succeeded by Lord Camden. Catholic Relief was thrown out by the Irish Parliament, the Government now declaring against it. Not contented with this, the Protestants began to organise themselves for the repression of the Catholics; the Catholics organised on their side; and the hatred of the rival races and creeds burst forth.

I have myself sought and found in the study of Irish history the explanation of the paradox, that a people with so many gifts, so amiable, naturally so submissive to rulers, and everywhere but in their own country industrious, are in their own country bywords of idleness, lawlessness, disaffection, and agrarian crime. But I will here follow Mr. Massey, not only one of the most matter-of-fact of writers,

but a most unquestionable enemy to revolution.
Mr. Massey writes thus : " Lord Carhampton,
the general commanding the forces in the disturbed districts, let loose his troops upon the
wretched peasantry. It was enough for a
magistrate, a squireen, or even a farmer to point
out any person as suspected, to have his habi-
tation burned down, his family turned adrift,
and himself either shot or transported, without
trial, without warrant, without inquiry. An
Act of Indemnity was passed by the Irish
Parliament, in the session of 1796, to protect
these enormities ; and the Insurrection Act
gave them for the future the sanction of law.
The suspension of the Habeas Corpus completed
this barbarous code, which, in effect, outlawed
the whole people of Ireland." The Government
armed a great body of Protestant yeomanry,
who were allowed to wear the Orange ribbon,
the badge of ascendancy. " The cruelties," says
Mr. Massey, " perpetrated by these men, both
before the rebellion, and while it was raging,
and after it was suppressed, differed only in
degree from the worst enormities of the French
revolutionists. Under the authority to search
for concealed arms, any person whom any

T 2

ruffian, calling himself a Protestant and a loyalist, and either with or without a military uniform, chose to suspect or to pretend to suspect, was liable to be seized, tortured, and put to death. Hundreds of unoffending people, and people who were guilty of no other offence than professing the creed of their fathers, and of letting fall a word of discontent, were flogged till they were insensible, or made to stand upon one foot on a pointed stake. These were the most ordinary punishments. Sometimes the wretched victim was half hanged, or the scalp was torn from the head by a pitched cap. Catholics and reputed malcontents of the better class were subjected to still worse treatment. Militia and yeomanry, as well as the regular troops, were billeted on them at free quarters; and this billet appears to have been invariably construed as an unlimited licence for robbery, devastation, ravishment, and, in case of resistance, murder."

Sir Ralph Abercromby, on assuming the command of the army in Ireland, branded these ruffians in general orders as formidable to everybody but the enemy. To him it did not appear essential to the honour of the profession that a

soldier should be licensed to play the butcher.
But he was at once hustled out of his command.
The Catholics, if they had not been goaded to
despair, would not have risen. Their priests had
no sympathy with the Atheists of the French
Republic. But the conduct of the Protestants
and of the Government drove them into the
arms of France and of the revolutionary conspirators of their own country, who were mostly
not Catholics, but Protestants, if they had any
religion at all. When the Catholic peasantry
did rise, they rose with the ruthless fury of
tortured and embruted slaves, and perpetrated
nameless atrocities in their turn. Then the
saturnalia of martial law were proclaimed;
and under cover of that proclamation, the vengeance of the dominant race was poured out,
as we have just seen the vengeance of a dominant race poured out, upon the victims of its
hate. Of that phrase martial law, absurd and
self-contradictory as it is, each part has a meaning. The term martial suspends the right of
citizens to legal trial; the term law suspends
the claim of an enemy to quarter and the other
rights of civilised war. The whole compound
is the fiend's charter; and the public man who

connives at its introduction, who fails in his day and in his place to resist it at whatever cost or hazard to himself, is a traitor to civilisation and humanity, and though official morality may applaud him at the time, his name will stand in history accursed and infamous for ever. The first notable case under martial law in Ireland was that of Sir Edward Crosbie, a gentleman residing near Carlow, where a rising had taken place. I will give the case in the words of Mr. Massey. " It unfortunately happened," says that writer, " that the miserable rabble, before entering the town, had paraded in the grounds of Sir Edward Crosbie, who resided at a distance of a mile and a half from Carlow. There was not a tittle of proof that this gentleman was in any way connected with the ˙rioters, or that he had invited them to assemble on his lawn at midnight, preparatory to their lawless proceedings. He had not accompanied them, nor did it appear that he held any communication with them. But Sir Edward was a friend to Parliamentary Reform, and hostile to the oppression of the tenantry by their landlords. To be friendly to the poor and to reform was presumptive evidence of disaffection;

and presumptive evidence of disaffection was
sufficient proof of complicity in the rebellion
The day after the attempt on Carlow several
persons were seized, tried by court-martial,
and hanged for this offence. Among others
Sir Edward Crosbie was dragged before a set
of ignorant, blood-thirsty ruffians, who styled
themselves a court-martial. There was not a
particle of evidence which could have had the
least weight with a fairly constituted court,
though Catholic prisoners had been, by torture
and promises of pardon, converted into witnesses against the accused. Numerous loyalists
came forward to state what everybody in the
neighbourhood knew, that Sir Edward was a
good subject of His Majesty, as well as one
of the few humane and accomplished gentlemen
that Ireland possessed. But these witnesses
were excluded from the place where the proceedings were held by the bayonets of the soldiery. A gentleman of rank and fortune, who
thought that Parliament should be reformed,
and that squireens should not be permitted
to grind and insult the peasantry, was a dangerous member of society, and must be made an
example of to deter others. Accordingly, Sir

Edward Crosbie was doomed to death by a court-martial, the president of which was an illiterate fellow who could not spell. The sentence was immediately put in execution at the gallows; and the remains of the murdered gentleman were abused in a manner shocking to humanity." The passages of history which derive their character from the lower and viler passions are apt to repeat themselves with great fidelity.

Lord Cornwallis, who had at length been sent over by Pitt, in the place of the wretched Camden, to stop these orgies of blood, states in one of his letters that under martial law "numberless murders are hourly committed without any process or examination whatever." "The yeomanry," he says, "are in the style of the loyalists in America, only much more numerous and powerful, and a thousand times more ferocious. These men have served their country, but they now take the lead in rapine and murder. The Irish militia, with few officers, and those chiefly of the worst kind, follow closely on the heels of the yeomanry in murder and every kind of atrocity; and the Fencibles take a share, although much behind-hand with

the others. The language of the principle
persons of the country all tends to encourage
this system of blood ; and the conversation, even
at my table, where you will suppose I do all I
can to prevent it, always turns on hanging, shoot-
ing, burning, etc. And if a priest has been
put to death, the greatest joy is expressed by
the whole company." He asserts from his own
knowledge of military affairs that of the numbers of the enemy reputed to be killed, a very
small proportion only are really killed in battle
—and adds that " he is afraid that any man
in a brown coat, who is found within several
miles of the field of action, is butchered without discrimination." He describes the principal
persons of the country and the members of both
Houses of Parliament as " averse to all acts of
clemency, and desiring to pursue measures that
would terminate in the extirpation of the inhabitants and the destruction of the country."
Lord Cornwallis was no friend of rebels : he had
commanded against rebels in America : he was
a Tory : he showed no weakness in quenching
the embers of the insurrection in Ireland. But
a burst of loyal execration arose against his
detestable clemency. Dr. Duiguenan, the organ

of the Orange party, wrote to Lord Castlereagh
that the conduct of the Lord-Lieutenant had
rendered him an object not only of disgust, but
of abhorrence to every loyal man. " You write,"
says Cornwallis to General Ross, " as if you
believed that there was any foundation for
all the lies and nonsensical clamour about my
lenity. On my arrival in this country, I put
a stop to the burning of houses and murder of
the inhabitants by the yeomen, or any other
person who delighted in that amusement; to
the flogging for the purpose of extorting
confession, and to the free quarters, which
comprehended universal rape and robbery
throughout the country." A party of the Mount
Kennedy corps of yeomanry (again I tell my
story in the words of Mr. Massey) were, on an
autumn night in the year 1798, patrolling the
village of Delbary, in the county of Wicklow.
Two or three of the party, led by Whollaghan,
one of their number, entered the cottage of a
labouring man named Dogherty, and asked
whether there were any bloody rebels there?
The only inmates of the cabin were Dogherty's
wife and a sick lad, her son, who was eating
his supper. Whollaghan asked if the boy was

Dogherty's son, and being told he was—"Then, you dog," said Whollaghan, "you are to die here." "I hope not," answered the poor lad; and he prayed, if there was any charge against him, to be taken before Mr. Latouche, a magistrate in the neighbourhood, of known humanity and justice. The fellow replied that he cared nothing for Latouche, and raised his gun. The mother entreated him, for the love of God, to take her life instead of her child's. Whollaghan, with a volley of abuse, pulled the trigger twice, but the piece missed fire. A comrade then handed him another gun; and the mother rushed at the muzzle to shield her son. In the struggle the piece went off, and the ball broke young Dogherty's arm. When the boy fell, the assassins left the cabin; but Whollaghan returned, and seeing the lad supported by his mother, cried out, "Is not the dog dead yet?" "Oh, yes, sir," said the poor woman, "he is dead enough." "For fear he is not," said Whollaghan, "let him take this." And with deliberate aim he fired a fourth time, and Dogherty dropped dead out of his mother's arms. Whollaghan was tried for

the murder, not by a civil tribunal as he
should have been, but by court-martial. The
facts were not disputed; but the defence was
that the poor boy had been a rebel, and that
the prisoner was a humane and loyal subject.
That the Doghertys were rebels is probable
enough; as indeed, says Mr. Massey, whom
I am still following, it was hardly possible
that a Catholic peasant could have been anything else. But no legal evidence of the fact
was tendered; and the hearsay, which was
admitted, was about as credible as the oaths
of the Orange-men who came to give Whollaghan a character for humanity. The real
defence was that the prisoner and his com-
panions had been sent out with general orders
to shoot anybody they pleased. "The court,"
remarks Mr. Massey, "seemed to have been
of opinion that such orders were neither
unusual or unreasonable; and it is difficult
to extract from their finding that they thought
the prisoner had been guilty even of an error
in judgment." They found that "the prisoner
did shoot and kill Thomas Dogherty, a rebel;
but acquitted him of any malicious or wilful
intention of murder."

Their sentiments seem, in fact, to have been pretty much the same as those which prevail in high official regions now. The trial took place at Dublin. The president of the court-martial was one of the leading members of that order who are the guardians of an honour and a morality above those of the common herd : he was the Earl of Enniskillen.

In Tipperary, Mr. Thomas Judkin Fitzgerald, a man of conspicuous loyalty, was made high-sheriff, and acted as a sort of provost-marshal in that district. His plan, says Mr. Massey, was to seize persons whom he chose to suspect, often without the slightest ground, if not from sheer malice, and by dint of the lash and threats of instant death, to extort confessions of guilt and accusations of other persons. He recommended himself especially to the approbation of all loyal men by attacking a somewhat higher class of persons than most of his compeers ventured to attack. Mr. Wright, a teacher of languages at Clonmel, and a man of good family, heard that he was suspected. He hastened to deliver himself up, in the hope that he might thus save his character and life. But Fitzgerald was not to

be disappointed of his victim. He received
Mr. Wright with a torrent of abuse, and ordered
him to fall on his knees to receive his sentence. "You are a rebel," said he, "and a
principal in this rebellion. You are to receive
five hundred lashes, and then to be shot."
The poor man begged for time, and was so
rash as to ask for a trial. This aroused Fitzgerald to fury; he railed at his prisoner for
daring to open his mouth after he was condemned. Wright was hurried to the flogging-
ladders, which were erected in the main street;
and expecting immediate death, had placed
his hat before his face while he muttered a
prayer. Fitzgerald with his own hand tore
away the hat, trampled on it, dragged his
fainting victim by the hair, kicked him, and
finally slashed him with a sword, drawing
blood. Wright was then fastened to the
ladder. Fifty lashes had been inflicted, when
a Major Riall came up and asked what Wright
had done. The Sheriff answered by flinging
Riall a note taken from the person of Wright,
as a justification of the punishment to which
he was subjected. The note was in French—
a language of which Fitzgerald was wholly

ignorant—and contained two lines excusing
the writer for having failed in a visiting
engagement. Riall assured Fitzgerald that
the note was perfectly harmless; nevertheless,
the lash continued to descend until the quiver-
ing entrails were visible through the flayed
flesh. The hangman was then ordered to
apply his thongs to a part of the body which
had not yet been torn, while the Sheriff
himself went to the general in command of
the district for an order to put his prisoner
to death. The order, however, was not given,
and Wright was released.

To add to the bright roll of English honour,
Mr. Thomas Judkin Fitzgerald received a pension, and, at the Union, was made a baronet
of the United Kingdom.

These men were not fiends; they were a
dominant class, the planter-class of Ireland,
maddened with cruel panic and administering
martial law. It is good that these things
should be recalled to mind when we see men
of letters and artists, who have been brought
up in the air of English liberty and within
the sound of Christian church bells, proposing
to blow Fenians from guns, and to re-enact

on Irish insurgents the atrocities which marked
the putting down of the Indian mutineers.

Ireland had what one of our prelates calls
a Missionary Church; that is an establishment profusely endowed out of the penury
and misery of the Irish people; and the
bishops and clergy of which were intended,
I suppose, to be placed by their wealth and
privileges above the passions of any class,
and enabled boldly to preach justice and
mercy. What were they doing? Were they
preaching justice and mercy, or were they
doing what the prelates and clergy of the
planter church of Jamaica do now—drawing
up certificates of Christian character for men
whose hands were red with innocent blood?
It is a point which I have never been able
clearly to ascertain.

There is nothing in this revolting history
more revolting than the cant about loyalty.
Loyalty is not due from the conquered and
the oppressed to the conqueror and oppressor.
Nothing is due but submission, which the
conqueror and oppressor must enforce as best
he can.

The Indemnity Act passed by the Irish

Parliament unfortunately proved insufficient to cover all these acts of the supporters of order, and especially the use of torture. Certain bloody-minded persecutors, pseudo-philanthropists, and Hiberno-philists were proceeding to appeal to the courts of law against indiscriminate butchery, torture, and arson. So the Parliament—of the temper and language of whose members, Lords and' Commons alike, we have heard Lord Cornwallis's description— passed a more comprehensive Act, which effectually screened every murderer, torturer, and incendiary from the law. Safe under this Act, Fitzgerald, when arraigned before a jury, vaunted his exploits in the face of justice. He named several persons whom he had flogged under circumstances more aggravated than those before the court. He mentioned one man who had cut his throat to escape the horrors and ignominy of torture. He admitted or boasted that in his search for rebels he had flogged many persons who had proved to be perfectly innocent. Lord Avonmore, who tried the case, did not dissemble his grief and indignation at having to administer such a law as that which had recently been enacted.

U

After dwelling on the flagrancy of the outrage, for which he said no damages would have been too great, he ended by saying that the words of the Act placed an insuperable bar between injury and redress, and set all equity and justice at defiance. And with that he dashed the Act upon the cushion, and threw himself back on his seat.

Lord Moira brought the state of things in Ireland before the British Legislature ; of course without effect. The Government supported their subordinates. If it is the duty of governments to support their subordinates, the people must support themselves. Statesmen are learning to make an easy reputation for chivalry by supporting their subordinates at the expense of humanity, justice, and the honour of the nation. Public morality requires that a subordinate should be supported in difficulty always, in error sometimes, in crime never.

Lord Stanhope charitably ascribes these horrors, in the refusal of all inquiry into which he apparently concurs, to a helpless crisis in human affairs, such as is described by the Cardinal de Retz, caused by accident and mischance, not by the faults or errors of mankind.

It was no helpless crisis, but the natural consequence of Protestant ascendancy in Ireland, sustained by the oligarchical government and hierarchy of this country. They were the authors before God of the Rebellion, though the people died for it by earthly law. And how far, I ask again, is the benefit of these excuses to extend? If ever the hand of fate was seen in history, it was in the history of the French Revolution. If ever a crisis could be called helpless, it was that of 1793. Is this to absolve the Jacobins? No; there have been misfortunes in Irish annals—misfortunes which were not faults—misfortunes which the rulers of Ireland in past times may fairly plead in their own excuse at the bar of history. The partial nature of the Anglo-Norman Conquest of Ireland, which led to the formation of an English pale instead of a national aristocracy mingling in course of time with the native race, was the original spring from which this bitterness flowed. But Protestant ascendancy was a fault, not a misfortune. And the obstinate maintenance in the interest of a class of an alien church and an alien land-law in Ireland are faults, not misfortunes, now. The guilt of the consequences in the eye of Heaven, rests on the Government, though still, by earthly law, the people pay the penalty.

The appearance of Hoche and his French armament of liberation in Bantry Bay was a warning which could not be neglected. Irish disaffection, if it is not formidable in itself, will always be formidable when it is backed by foreign aid. If Hoche had landed, he would, for the time at least, have been master of Ireland. The Orange yeomanry and militia, though they could murder, burn, and torture, could not stand before an enemy, as they showed when they were led against the small French force afterwards landed by Humbert. And with steam instead of sails Hoche would have landed. It had become manifest that the Orange government of Ireland was not only criminal but dangerous. Pitt now resolved to carry the Union, and the Union was carried. It was carried through an Irish Parliament in which the Irish people were not represented, and which had no sort of right or title to dispose of the independence of the nation. And through that Parliament it was carried by bribery and corruption of every kind, including the prostitution of honours and offices as well as pensions, so foul and infamous that men of honour, such as Lord Cornwallis, who were employed in the operation, shrank with loathing from their task. One million two hundred and sixty thousand pounds were distributed among the proprietors of boroughs as compensation for the loss of their means of preying on the State, and the peerage was again recruited with houses which derive from this noble origin their divine right of legislating for the nation. The acquiescence of the Catholics was procured by fraud ; the hope of emancipation was distinctly held out to them as the price of their concurrence, and was not fulfilled. The Union was a good and an indispensable measure. It was, as Pitt saw, the only chance of saving Ireland from Protestant ascendancy and provincial tyranny : and legally of course it is perfectly valid. To give it moral validity, it requires the free ratification of the Irish people. When the Union is what Pitt declared it was to be, a union of equal laws, that ratification will be obtained.

Pitt is generally held to have been a bad war minister. That he was not a successful war minister is certain : and in war, if in anything, ministers may be judged by their success. His navy gained victories by dint of British seamanship and courage. His military operations ended almost uniformly in disaster. His forces were never found on a decisive field. Like a bad chess-player he ran over the board taking pawns, while the adversary was checking his king. He carried his victorious arms from Tobago to St. Domingo, from St. Domingo to St. Lucia, and from St. Lucia to Guadaloupe. This was the traditional mode of making war on France ; and he did not see how different was the France on which he had now to make war. Meantime his allies were being beaten in battles, which, if they had been won, would have given him as many sugar islands as he pleased ; and which, being lost, swept away the sugar islands in the general ruin. When Bonaparte and the best army of France were in Egypt and off the board, Pitt took advantage of their absence, not to join his allies in dealing a decisive blow, but to make an isolated descent on the enemy's country, the weakest operation in proportion to

the force employed which can be undertaken,
and one which in this case ended in ignominious
failure. He had not his father's eye for men.
Chatham would have brought Nelson to the
front before. When Nelson had won the Nile,
Pitt only gave him the lowest rank in the peerage, and said, in defence of this parsimony in
rewarding merit, that Nelson would live as the
winner of the greatest of naval victories, and
that no one would ask whether he had been
made a baron, a viscount, or an earl. This,
when the highest rank in the peerage was being
every day bestowed on political subserviency,
and even on political corruption : when Sir
James Lowther was made an earl direct for his
influence at Appleby. Pitt is open to a worse
censure that that of merely failing to distinguish merit. When he allowed himself to be
made minister by an unconstitutional use of the
King's personal influence, he had sold himself to
the fiend, and the fiend did not fail to exact the
bond. Twice Pitt had the criminal weakness to
gratify the King's personal wishes by entrust-
ing the safety of English armies and the honour
of England to the incompetent hands of the
young Duke of York. This absurd princeling

actually objected to acting under the command
of Clarifait, the most competent and eminent of
the allied generals : and to gratify his conceit,
the command-in-chief was assumed by the Emperor, the arch-incompetency of all. But, after
all, could promotion by merit be expected at the
hands of governments whose essence was privilege ? It was against promotion by merit that
they were fighting. To accept promotion by
merit would have been to accept the revolution.

In the sixth year of the war, the nation was
brought to the brink of destruction by a mutiny
in the fleet, caused entirely by the vices of the
administration. The pay of the sailors and their
pensions had not been increased since the time
of Charles II., in spite of the immense rise of
prices since that period, which must have been
felt more than ever in time of war. This, while
millions were being paid to boroughmongers and
sinecurists, and when Tomline was not satisfied
unless he had a rich bishopric and a rich deanery
too. Light weight of provisions was served, a
sailor's pound being fourteen ounces instead of
sixteen ; and even for this short weight the
sailors were dependent on pursers taken from a
low class, who cheated them without limit. The

distribution of prize-money was most unfair ; the
discipline most vexatious ; the officers, who were
appointed entirely by interest, were incompetent
and tyrannical ; and seamen who had fought the
battles of the country, seamen scarred with honourable wounds, were sworn at and abused like
dogs by insolent and worthless boys. At last
the sailors rose and respectfully demanded redress. The Government, conscious of its guilt,
was compelled to accede to their demands, and
even to dismiss a number of officers from the
service. But the spirit of mutiny once roused,
naturally broke forth again in a more turbulent
and dangerous form. It was suppressed at last,
and justice of course was done on the principal
mutineers, who were hanged or flogged through
the fleet. It must be owned, however, that even
in the case of the worst offenders, justice was
tempered with mercy, for no lord of the Admiralty was either flogged or hanged. Since that
time, and owing originally to the mutiny, the
navy has been in a sounder state. Neither that
nor any service will be in a perfectly sound state
till dismissal is the highest punishment. And
now—Democracy is such an ungrateful thing—
can any one point out to us an instance in

history, from Athens down to the American
Republic, in which a Democracy treated its
defenders as the British seaman was treated
before the mutiny at Spithead? Democracy
does not build Blenheims and create vast estates
for the general or the admiral; but it is just,
and it cannot help being just, to the soldier
and the sailor.

What Pitt's war finance was, tax-payers need
not to be told. He did make an effort to keep
borrowing within bounds, but it soon broke
down, and he plunged headlong into an abyss
of debt. In this he was backed by a Parliament
of the rich and idle trained to public extravagance by prodigality at home. His own recklessness in private expenditure is too well known.
It compelled him to accept somewhat ignominious aid. This system of laying burdens on
posterity removes, as I have said before, the
last check on war. Nor is it capable of moral
defence. The theory on which Pitt and his
supporters acted—that they had a right to
mortgage the estate which they bequeathed to
posterity—assumed that the earth belonged
to one generation of men. The earth does
not belong to one generation of men, but to

God, who has given it to each generation in its turn.

Of Pitt's war taxes the most notable were the income-tax and the succession-tax. The income-tax is a tax which ought to be resorted to only in time of war or in some national emergency which excites the national spirit as much as war. It is only when the national spirit is so excited that there is a chance of true returns. In ordinary times the income-tax is a tax on honesty, a premium on dishonesty, a corruptor of national and especially of commercial honour. Pitt proposed a succession duty on real and personal property alike ; but the landlord Parliament threw out the duty on real property, and passed that on personal property alone. There are no Trades Unions in the House of Commons.

Pitt had gone into the war reckoning on the failure of the French finances. While French finance was recruited by despair, he was driven to a suspension of cash payments. There is no great mystery, I apprehend, about the character and effects of this measure. It was, in fact, a forced loan, which was paid off, at the expense of great national suffering, by the return to cash payments after the war. Meantime it caused a depreciation of the currency, which bore hard on fixed incomes, while it did not affect the landowners, whose rents could be raised.

All political progress was, of course, suspended in England, as it was over Europe generally, in these disastrous years. Pitt's speeches were full of claptrap against democracy, as though Equality were responsible for the political calamities which Privilege had brought on in France. He now openly renounced Parliamentary Reform, and began to declaim in the full Tory strain against following false luminaries and abandoning the polestar of the British constitution. He and his party maintained that the rotten borough Parliament, the stench of whose corruption rose to heaven, which was wasting the blood and substance of the people in a class war, and brutalising them at the same time, had been found amply sufficient for securing their happiness, and that the system ought not to be idly and wantonly disturbed, from any love of experiment, or predilection for theory. It would be very wrong to do anything wantonly or idly, or from mere love of experiment, or predilection for theory. But supposing that an absurd system of representation did work well, not only for those who monopolise power and patronage under it, and who of course find it practically excellent, but for the nation : still its absurdity would be an evil calling for amendment, because institutions ought to command the reverence of the people, which they cannot do unless they are intelligible and consistent with reason. And if theory is nothing, and if the people are already practically represented, where is the great danger of bringing the theory into accordance with the practice ? Great allowance is to be made for the Tory Minister in this matter : but had he been one of the first of statesmen, he would have seen how sure an antidote against disaffection and foreign contagion was to be found in timely and moderate Reform.

It has been said that when Pitt had once gone into the war, he ought to have made it a crusade. Burke complained at the time that he did not : and the charge has been repeated with great amplitude of rhetoric by Lord Macaulay. If Pitt did not actually proclaim a crusade, he used language about the salvation of Europe wild enough to satisfy most fanatics, and the flagitious nonsense which he did not talk himself, he allowed his colleagues and

subordinates to talk for him. So far as he re-
strained himself or them, he is to be praised,
as Lord Stanhope justly says, for not having
given the war a character which would have
made it internecine. But as to a crusade, who
were to be the crusaders? Would the boroughmongers and the sinecurists have played the
part of Tancred and Godfrey? Would Tomline
and Dr. Cornwallis have gone forth, like the
bishops of the middle ages, at the head of the
army of the Cross? Burke himself, the Peter the
Hermit of this crusade, would he have left Bea-
consfield and his pension to share the doom of
those whom he had sent forth to die? Save the
Sepulchre! Save Gatton and Old Sarum! Save
the Earldom of Lonsdale, save the Clerkship of
the Pells, the Wardenship of the Cinque Ports,
the Tellership of the Exchequer, the salaries of
the Six Clerks, and the Deputy Chafe-wax!
Save the Deanery of St. Paul's and "the only
arrangement which can offer any accommodation in my favour!" Crusading is self-sacrifice.
These men were carrying on a war in their own
interest, with armies of peasants trepanned by
drink and the recruiting sergeant, with seamen
levied by the press-gang, and with the money

of future generations. They had not self-sacrifice enough even to suppress for the moment their own petty jealousies and interested intrigues for office in the most desperate moments of the struggle. The ruling class, I apprehend, bore little of the burden. If their taxes rose, their rents and tithes rose also ; and they shared a vast mass of patronage besides. The great merchants who supported the war were in like manner growing rich, as great merchants in war often do, at the expense of their less opulent rivals. Burke had described them on a former occasion as snuffing with delight the cadaverous scent of lucre. The crusading spirit, if it was anywhere, was on the side of the French youths, who went forth shoeless and ragged, without pay, with nothing but bread and gunpowder, to save their country from the Coalition, and, as some of them thought, to overthrow tyranny of body and soul, and open a new reign of justice and happiness for mankind. When the French Revolution had turned to the lust of military aggrandisement embodied in Bonaparte, the crusading spirit passed to the other side, and then the leaders of England might appeal to it not in vain.

Pitt did not know why he had gone to war, and therefore when he found himself abandoned by most of his allies, the rest requiring subsidies to drag them into the field, the cause of Europe, as it was called, thus renounced by Europe itself, everything going ill, and no prospect of amendment, he did not know how or on what terms to make peace. This is called his firmness. He vaguely represented himself as fighting for security for the past and reparation for the future, and his words were parroted by his party; but it was not stated what the reparation or the security was. He pretended at one time that there was no government in France with which a treaty could be made. There was always a government in France, even during the Reign of Terror, obeyed by the nation and the national functionaries, and with which, therefore, a treaty might have been made. It signifies nothing, as everybody would now admit, how polluted the origin or character of a foreign government may be, you must treat with it as a government. If its origin and character are polluted, or even questionable, you need not, and if you are jealous of the honour of your country and your own you will not,

fling England into its arms, or eagerly place
her hand in the hand which has been held up
to heaven in perjury and is stained with innocent blood. But you must treat all governments as governments; it is the only way of
fixing responsibility where circumstances not
under your control have fixed power.

Pitt, however, finding disasters thickening,
did struggle to make peace. He underwent
great humiliations to obtain it. His envoys
waited, with a submissiveness and a patience
which must call a blush to every English cheek,
in the antechambers of the insolent and domi-
neering Directory. He even offered to pay two
of the Directors the heavy bribe which they
demanded. England trying to bribe two
sharpers to vouchsafe her a peace! But the
profligate lust of aggrandisement which had
now taken the place of defensive objects in
the councils of the French Government, the
insufferable temper of its chiefs, the divisions
in the Directory between the Jacobins and the
party of Reaction, and at the same time the
divisions in the English Cabinet between Pitt,
who was for peace, and Grenville, who was
still for war, prolonged the bloodshed and the

misery for eight years.   At last, in 1801, peace,
and an ignominious peace, was inevitable.   Pitt
has been suspected of having slipped out of
office and put Addington in to eat the dirt,
meaning himself to return to power when the
dirt had been eaten.   There seems to be no
ground for the suspicion, though Pitt's conduct at this juncture is not easy to understand.   The ostensible cause of Pitt's retirement
was the King's refusal to allow him to redeem
the pledge which he had given to the Catholics
at the time of the Irish Union.   Not only was
his honour involved, but it was of vital importance to the nation, engaged in a desperate
struggle, that the estrangement of the Irish,
from whom a large proportion of our soldiers
were drawn, should be brought to an end.   But
the King had a conscience.   Pitt resigned, putting in his friend and creature, Addington,
merely, as I am convinced, to keep his place for
him till the Catholic difficulty could be solved.
" Mr. Pitt," said Sir James Graham, speaking
of the Catholic Emancipation, " was prepared
to do the right thing at the right moment ; but
genius gave way to madness, and two generations have deplored the loss of an opportunity

which never will return." Genius gave way to
madness, but to madness practised upon by
genius of another kind. The chief performer
was Lord Loughborough, of whom when he
died His Majesty was pleased to say (having
first assured himself that the melancholy news
was true) "that a greater rogue was not
left in his dominions." Loughborough's coadjutor was Auckland, afterwards spurned as a
knavish intriguer both by Pitt and by the King.
Their instruments in tampering with the conscience of the half-insane King were Moore,
Archbishop of Canterbury, the odour of whose
nepotism has reached the nostrils even of our
generation, and the Primate of Ireland, who
was called in as a wolf to decide this question
of conscience as to the claims of the sheep.
There is scarcely a worse intrigue in history.

And now came a strange turn of affairs.
Scarcely was Pitt out and Addington in, when
Pitt sent the King a promise never to moot the
question of Catholic Emancipation again during
his life. Not only so, but he undertook, in case
any one else should moot the question, to find the
means of setting it aside. The reason alleged for
this strange sacrifice of a pledge and a principle,

was that the agitation of the King's mind on the subject had brought on a recurrence of his illness. If this was true, we may remark, in the first place, that here is another warning to nations in search of a constitution ; and, in the second place, that if the state of the King's mind was such that he could not consider a State question of the most vital and pressing impoitance without bringing on derangement, he was physically unfit for the duties of his office, and he ought to have given place to a Regent. Lord Stanhope urges the claim of His Majesty's conscience to loyal forbearance, but perhaps he does not sufficiently consider, on the other hand, the claim of the nation to existence. The doctrine that one man ought to die for the people has been propounded, though not by auspicious lips ; but no one has yet propounded the doctrine that the people ought to die for one man. Not only George III., but his highly conscientious son and successor, had scruples about Catholic Emancipation and the Coronation oath : and George the Fourth's successor might have had the same. This is not constitutional government. What great measure of reform would ever have been carried, if it had required the free personal

assent of the Sovereign and the majority of the
House of Lords ?   George III. was against the
abolition of the slave-trade.   Were the horrors
of the middle passage to go on while he lived ?
But the fact is, his conscience was not a God-
made conscience, it was a bishop-made and chan-
cellor-made conscience ; and it had not the firmness any more than the purity of the God-made.
It would have given way under vigorous pressure, as it always did.   He had ordered his yacht
for Hanover more than once ; but he counter-
manded it when people were firm.

One thing, at all events, ought to have been
done.   The secret intriguers against justice and
the safety of the nation ought to have been
dragged into the light of day, and made personally responsible for the advice which they had
given the King.   But how could Pitt do this—
he who had allowed himself to be made Prime
Minister by the secret and equally infamous intrigue between the King and Temple ?   The
fiend always claims his bond.

The situation, however, was now absurd.   Pitt
was out, though by his abandonment of the
Catholic cause the sole ostensible ground of his
retirement had been removed : Addington was

in, equally without reason. Of course Pitt's
friends wished at once to take out the warming-
pan and put back the man. But to do this was
now not easy. The warming-pan did not know
that it was a warming-pan. It had been told
by Pitt when he put it in that it was the man
of the crisis. It took the flatterer at his word.
It grew settled and self-satisfied in place. The
King, who had revered the august Pitt, was
attracted with magnetic force to the comfortable
mediocrity of Addington. He addressed him in
the most affectionate terms—" The King cannot
find words sufficiently expressive of His Majesty's
cordial approbation of the whole arrangements
which *his own* Chancellor of the Exchequer has
wisely, and His Majesty chooses to add most
correctly recommended." Pitt himself, though
clearly conscious of the disarrangement, was, for
a long time, forbearing : he had enough to rest
on : but his younger friends were more impatient. Canning lampooned Addington, who had
a brother named Hiley, and a brother-in-law
named Bragge :—

> " When the faltering periods lag,
>   When the House receives them drily,
> Cheer, oh, cheer him, Brother Bragge,
>   Cheer, oh, cheer him, Brother Hiley."

And again, when the Thames was being fortified with blockhouses :—

> " If blocks can from danger deliver,
>   Two places are safe from the French,
> The one is the mouth of the river,
>   The other the Treasury bench."

The same active and ingenious spirit proposed to present to Addington a round-robin, telling him how much everybody wished him to resign ; and as there was a difficulty in getting the best signatures, Canning suggested that the round-robin should be sent in without signatures, and that Addington should be told that he could have the signatures if he liked. It was proposed that Addington, as being Speaker was his specialty, should be made Speaker of the House of Lords ; they would have made him Speaker of Elysium if that place had been vacant. For three years all the world was out of joint, and everybody was in perplexity. Mr. Wilberforce wrote in his diary : " I am out of spirits, and doubtful about the path of duty in these political battles. I cannot help regretting that Addington's temperance and conciliation should not be connected with more vigour." And then he puts up a prayer to Heaven for guidance. Heaven,

I suspect, left these politicians pretty much to themselves.

At last necessity, which will have the man and not the warming-pan, came in the shape of the renewal of the war with a danger of invasion. A little subterranean work was done by the Lord Chancellor Eldon, and Addington found himself and his friends gently lifted out of place, and Pitt quietly installed in their room, Eldon remaining Chancellor in the new administration. Lord Eldon's conduct in this matter, of which many hard things have been said, has been a good deal cleared by Lord Stanhope. Addington, it appears, authorised the Chancellor to open negotiations, and all that can be said is, that he was not kept informed of their progress, and was by no means gratified at their result. Eldon thought himself above the rules. He was the King's own Chancellor, not a mere member of ephemeral administrations. Had not the King, when the Chancellor was appointed, buttoned up the great seal in the breast of his coat, and taking it out said—" I give it you from my heart?" However, after the light thrown upon the transaction by Lord Stanhope, we are happy to acquiesce in His Majesty's intimation to "his excellent Lord Chancellor," that "the uprightness of Lord Eldon's mind, and his attachment to the King, have borne him with credit and honour, and (what the King knows will not be without its due weight) with the approbation of his Sovereign, through an unpleasant labyrinth." The last two words at all events are true.

Pitt came in to conduct a war, and this time a necessary war; for I am convinced that with the perfidy and rapine of Bonaparte no peace could be made, that the struggle with him was a struggle for the independence of all nations against the armed and disciplined hordes of a conqueror as cruel and as barbarous as Attila. The outward mask of civilisation Bonaparte wore, and he could use political and social ideas for the purposes of his ambition as dexterously as cannon; but in character he was a Corsican and as savage as any bandit of his isle. If utter selfishness, if the reckless sacrifice of humanity to your own interest and passions be vileness, history has no viler name. I can look with pride upon the fortitude and constancy which England displayed in the contest with the universal tyrant. The position in which it left her at its close was fairly won : though she must now be content to retire from this temporary supremacy, and fall back into her place as one of the community of nations. But Pitt was still destined to fail as a war minister ; and Trafalgar was soon cancelled by Austerlitz. "How I leave my country !" Such, it seems, is the correct version of Pitt's last words. Those words are perhaps his truest epitaph. They express the anguish of a patriot who had wrecked his country.

APPENDIX.

APPENDIX.

THE ANCIENT FREEHOLDERS OF ENGLAND.

THE number of the Buckinghamshire freeholders who brought up the Petition in favour
of Hampden, and to whom reference is made
in the lecture on Pym, was variously estimated
at the time; by themselves it was placed as
high as six thousand, by their enemies as low
as two thousand. (See Mr. Forster's "Arrest
of the Five Members," p. 353, note.) Rushworth
(iv. p. 487) says:—"This day divers knights,
gentlemen, and freeholders of the County of
Bucks, to the number of about four thousand
(as they were computed), came to London,
riding every one with a printed copy of the
Protestation lately taken in his hat." Clarendon
says:—"As soon as the citizens and mariners
were discharged, some Buckinghamshire men,

who were said to be at the door with a
petition, and had, indeed, waited upon the
triumph with a train of several thousand men,
were called in; who delivered their petition
in the name of the inhabitants of the County
of Buckingham, and said it was brought to
the town by about six thousand men."

In "Whitelocke's Memorials" (vol. iv. p. 272)
there is an entry respecting the writer's election
as a knight of the shire for Buckingham, which
throws some light on the number of the freeholders. "At the election of the knights of
the shire for Bucks, my friends marched into
Bucks one thousand horse, and were in the
field above three thousand, so that I was
first and unanimously elected, and with me
Colonel Ingoldsby, Sir Richard Piggott, Mr.
Hambden (the son of the great man), and
Mr. Granville." This was under Cromwell's
Reform Act, embodied in the Instrument of
Government, which gave votes for counties not
only to freeholders, but to all persons holding
property, by whatever tenure, to the value of
£200; so that probably many leaseholders and
copyholders took part in the election. On the
other hand, those who had fought for the

King since the commencement of the troubles were disabled from voting; and in the divided state of the other party, consequent on the quarrel between the Presbyterians and Independents, it is not likely that all the electors who remained qualified would come forward to vote for a man connected as Whitelocke was with the Protector. Not a few of the wives of the freeholders who rode up to London to support Hampden must have been widows. Whitelocke's words seem to imply that the other candidates had their special cavalcades of adherents as well as himself, though they may have been less numerous than his own. We may feel pretty sure, from the habits of life prevalent at that time, that the bulk of these electors were really Buckinghamshire men resident on the holdings which formed their electoral qualifications.

Whitelocke gives this account of the Ironsides: —" Cromwell had a brave regiment of horse of his countrymen, most of them *freeholders and freeholder's sons*, and who upon matter of conscience engaged in this quarrel. And thus being well armed within by the satisfaction of their own consciences, and without by good iron arms, they would as one man stand firmly and fight desperately."

M. Guizot, in his "History of the English Revolution," notices the subdivision of land and the increase of the different classes of resident proprietors as characteristic of the period of Charles I., ascribing them, in part, to the breaking up of the great Church estates, which had been granted to courtiers, by whose prodigality they were dispersed, and to the sale of Crown lands enforced by the fiscal necessities of the Crown.

There seems to be no doubt that in the seventeenth century, and even at a later period, England contained a much larger number than at present of yeomen freeholders subsisting by the cultivation of their own land. The character of these men appears to be very distinctly marked upon the history of our revolution. They are the heart and the sinews of the Puritan cause. In ordinary times they accept the leadership of the higher gentry, as the lists of Parliament show : but they have independent opinions of their own : it is upon matter of conscience that they engage in the quarrel; and when the aristocracy desert the cause they stand firm to it, adhere to a leader of their own class, and bear him on to victory. An independent yeomanry has left a similar mark in the history of other countries, where that class has borne the brunt of patriotic or religious struggles, and most recently and signally in the history of the United States, where the yeomen, especially those of the west, were, throughout the late struggle with the slave-owners, the unshaken pillars of the Republic. The farmer, though less active-minded, of course, than the trader or the artizan, is, as a general rule, more meditative, has more depth of character, and, when a principle comes home to him, grasps it more firmly. But to make his spirit independent, he should be the owner of his own land.

The remnant of these yeomen still lingers, under the name of "statesmen," in Cumberland and Westmoreland, where they formed, in the language of Wordsworth, "a perfect republic of shepherds and agriculturists, proprietors for the most part of the land which they occupied and cultivated." But from the rest of England they have either altogether disappeared, or are very rapidly disappearing. Such, at least, is the

Y

conviction of all whom I have been able to consult, whether general economists or persons of local knowledge and experience. We have, unfortunately, no published statistics, of a trustworthy kind, as to the proprietorship of land, and the changes which it has been undergoing.

Mr. Disraeli, indeed, in the speech in which he attacked the passage in the text, boasted that there were still four thousand freeholders upon the electoral register of Bucks, and he implied that these were freeholders of the old yeoman class, part of " the backbone of the country." There are not only four thousand freeholders on the register, but four thousand five hundred, the number having recently increased. But an inspection of the register at once indicates, and local inquiry decisively confirms the indication, that, for the most part, these are not freeholders of the old yeoman kind. Of the 4,500, 2,100 only are at once occupiers and owners ; and of the holdings of these 2,100, more than half are at an estimated rental of less than £14. The holdings of a large proportion are in towns, as Mr. Disraeli himself is always complaining, and belong to a class of electoral nuisance which he is always scheming to clear away from the fair face of the rural creation. The descriptions of the properties in the electoral register are not precise, but when inspected, and compared with the electors' places of abode, it will be found that they are seldom suggestive of a freehold farm cultivated by a resident owner.*

---

* In speaking of this question at Guildford, I took as a specimen the electoral register of the parish of Chalfont St. Giles, Bucks, not because I had or pretended to have any local information as to that parish, but as I stated at the time, because it happened to be the first rural parish in the register of the county. I believe I gave the analysis correctly. But there appears to be some discrepancy, not only between the electoral register and the actual list of landholders in the parish, some of whom are females, or register their votes in other parishes, but between the impressions of local informants as to the character of some of the holdings and their occupants. The Rector, who challenged my statement in a published letter, makes 10, and according to a list with which he has since favoured me, even 13 "homesteads," while another informant thinks that the designation of "yeoman subsisting by the cultivation of his own land" can be properly applied only to two holders, whose farms together comprise but 82 acres out of a total acreage of 3,550. The last-mentioned informant also states, and is supported by other persons acquainted with the district in the statement, that the class of freeholders which existed in Hampden's days is quietly disappearing from that part

The change is due, no doubt, mainly to economical causes independent of legislation. Wealth has of late years accumulated to an immense extent in commercial hands, and the

of the country. It is useless, however, to carry on a discussion respecting a single disputed instance, when the general fact is undisputed. I only wish to remark that my assertions were not "random:" they were an account of a document before me, to which Mr. Disraeli had appealed.

In the same speech (or, as I should rather call it, epilogue to my lecture) I alluded, in passing, to the connection of Milton with Chalfont St. Giles. My words I believe were, "There Milton found a refuge, at the time when Mr. Disraeli's party was in the ascendant." This seems to have been turned, in an abridged report, into "Thither Milton fled from the Tory mercies of the Restoration." The Rector thereupon reminded me with some asperity that Milton had left London to avoid the plague, and that he was secured against personal danger by the Act of Indemnity. Milton left London to avoid the plague; but he came to Chalfont, I apprehend, because in that district the Hampden and Cromwell connection was very strong, and he would there be safe from annoyances against which no Act of Indemnity could secure him. (See Murray's Handbook for Bucks, under *Amersham.*) My real words imported no more. Milton, however, did not feel himself quite so safe as the Rector of Chalfont thinks.

> "On evil days though fallen and evil tongues ;
> In darkness, and *with dangers compassed round*
> And solitude."

first ambition of its possessors generally is to invest it in land. Prices are thus offered for land which the smaller holders cannot resist. The high prices of the French war led land-owners into extravagance which, when peace and the fall of prices arrived, probably compelled the sale of many a yeoman's or small gentleman's estate. The habits of the farmer class generally, and of their families, have become more luxurious and expensive, and the produce of a small holding has not sufficed for their desires. Money has also been borrowed for improvements, and the land has gone in the end to pay the debt. The running out of the leases on the Church and College estates has converted a considerable number of holdings which were practically almost freeholds into tenancies at will.

It seems impossible, however, that entails, or to speak more accurately family settlements, and the law of primogeniture in succession to intestates, which though seldom operative itself, leads the custom, should not greatly contribute to prevent the subdivision of land. Cases have been mentioned to me in which a subdivision has evidently followed upon the disentailment of a great estate, among others that of the great Buckingham estate, the disentailment of which, as I am informed, has brought into existence a considerable number of smaller proprietors.*

I shall not attempt here to enter into the economical part of the question. All the ordinary laws of human nature must be reversed with regard to this subject, if security of tenure is not conducive to the progress of agriculture, provided that the holder has wherewithal to improve the land. It can scarcely be thought possible that land, if it continues to bear anything like its present price, can pass to any considerable extent into the hands of peasant proprietors : but if thrown into a free market, it might pass to some extent into the hands of smaller holders subsisting by agriculture, and from whom active and successful farming might be expected.

* I have been understood as saying that *five hundred* freeholders have been called into existence by the breaking up of the Buckingham estates. But this is a mistake. What I said was, that five hundred had been added to the number of the Buckinghamshire freeholders on the electoral register, and that the recent increase, as I was informed, was *partly* caused by the breaking up of the Buckingham estate.

In a political point of view, the country has reason to lament the loss of a worthy and independent class of citizens. The most independent class now are the skilled artisans ; but the skilled artisans, with all their intelligence, have not the political any more than they have the physical robustness of the yeoman : and moreover they are not, like the yeomen, a military power.

In a social point of view the absence of so many of the great proprietors from their estates, either wholly or during the London season, and the immense interval between them and the mass of the labouring population, are great drawbacks from the civilising influence which they are supposed to exercise. It is open to inquiry, at all events, whether a body of proprietors, tolerably educated, always resident and always in immediate contact with the labourer, might not be a beneficial supplement to the squire and the tenant-farmer, the squire pressing the tenant, the tenant pressing those beneath him.

Let artificial restrictions, such as the unnatural privilege of tying up land to persons not in being, be removed ; let land be brought freely into the market; and all inducements and influences will, in the course of nature, have their just weight and find their proper level. Such, in every point of view, is the dictate of the general good, whatever the desire of maintaining a territorial aristocracy for political purposes may have to say upon the other side.